DARK RÛNA

DARK RÛNA

Containing the Complete Essays Originally Published
in
BLACK RÛNA
(1995)
with
Additional Content

Stephen Edred Flowers

Copyright © 2019
by Runestar LLC

All rights reserved. No part of this book, either in part or in whole, may be reproduced, transmitted or utilized in any form or by any means electronic, photographic or mechanical, including photocopying, recording, or by any information storage and retrieval system, without the permission in writing from the Publisher, except for brief quotations embodied in literary articles and reviews.

For permissions, or for the serialization, condensation, or for adaptation write the Publisher at the address below.

Published by
Runestar
P.O. Box 16
Bastrop, Texas 78602

Preface 2019

The original edition of *Black Rûna* was published in 1995 and was limited to 504 signed copies. These sold out fairly quickly. I said I would never reprint this edition, and I have not done so here. The new title of the collection accounts for the limited nature and collectable value of the original 1995 edition. The problem has become that many people want to see the contents of this book and I felt obligated to make it available. Since much of the lore relating to Temple of Set and Order of the Trapezoid has since been published under the imprimatur of the Temple of Set and disseminated to the public, there is certainly no motive to keep this material more restricted in its availability than it needs to be.

Many of the articles have additional notes added in the 1995 edition. These are included in square brackets. Other additional notes added in this edition follow these with the date 2019, also in square brackets.

The original dedication page to the 1995 version of this text read:

> for Lady Lance, a valkyrie among us,
> for Sir Setnakt, who blazes a trail to the south,
> for Sir Rudra, who blazes a trail to the east,
> for Sir CuChulainn who blazes a trail to the west,
> for Dame Pat who shows us the stars,
>
> and for Sir Michael, who showed us all the way
> and whose *sverðtakari* I am.

Each of these individuals went on to have illustrious careers and accomplishments. Two of them eventually became the High Priest or High Priestess of Set and Grand Master of the Order of the Trapezoid. One became an attorney and another a distinguished professor.

For this edition, I would also like to acknowledge the contributions of Sir Saturnus, the present Grand Master of the Order of the Trapezoid and author of the book *Infernal Geometry* (Inner Traditions, 2019).

Abbreviations

BCE	Before the Common Era (= B.C.)
CE	Common Era (= A.D.)
ch.	chapter
CTL	Command to Look
DeV	*Die elektrischen Vorspiele*
GBM	Greater Black Magic
LBM	Lesser Black Magic
NS	National Socialism
NSDAP	*Nationalsozialistische deutsche Arbeiterpartei* (National Socialist German Workers' Party
ON	Old Norse
O.Tr.	Order of the Trapezoid
O∴T∴	Order of the Trapezoid
UFA	Universal Film A.G.

Contents

Preface (2019) v
Introduction (1995) 1
Mysteries of the Graal (1985) 11
On the Way of Wotan and the Left-Hand Path (1985) 25
The Command to Look (1986) 17
Trapezoidal Runology (1986) 23
Runes and Angles (1986) 31
Graal Mythos in Old English Runes? (1986) 33
Runic Origins of the "Peace Sign" (1986) 35
Set and Wotan (1986) 37
Walburga in Khem (1986) 41
Trapezoidal Cinema (1987) 43
Austin Osman Spare and the Track of the Trapezoid (1987) 47
Magie und Manipulation (1987) 51
A Root of the "Occult Nazi Mythos" Review of *The Occult Causes of the Present War* (1987) 61
Infernal Contraptions (1987) 63
Galdr ok Seiðr (1988) 67
Nazi Occultism Revisited (1988) 69
On the Choice of a Human Sacrifice... (1989) 75
Addendum 2019: Meditation on the Seal of Rûna 81
Bibliography 83
Notice 85

Introduction
to *Black Rûna* (1995)

I

What you have before you is an anthology of contributions I made to the official internal organ of the Order of the Trapezoid within the Temple of Set. These were published between the years 1985 and 1989. Many of the articles have to do with some aspect of the Northern tradition of magic and initiation— but from the unique angle of the Left-Hand Path.

Black Rûna is designed to allow the general public some access to the genuine ideological and magical world of the Order of the Trapezoid— which I hope will dispel much of the inflammatory nonsense that has been written about this noble Order in the tabloid-type press.

My own involvement with the O.Tr. began at some point in the remote past. But from a historical perspective, my involvement came with my own founding of an order which I called "The Order of the Shining Trapezoid." The O.S.T. was founded on November 11, 1983. It was an attempt on my part to make contact with the "dark side" of Odinism, the dark and *futuristic* side of the Northern Way, which my own academic studies and personal intuition had told me was there— and Necessary. The founding of the O.S.T. acted as a magical catalyst to open a gate in the objective universe. Within a few weeks, I learned of the Temple of Set through a text which obliquely referred to the Temple's studies in Germanic occultism of this century. Shortly thereafter, on January 13, 1984, I wrote a letter to the Temple of Set. The response from the Temple convinced me at once that *this* was the gate to the dark side I had tried to open myself just a few weeks before. For once I would not have to do *all* the Work myself.

On February 7, 1984, I was accepted as a Setian I°, and ten days later, in an unprecedented move, I was also accepted as a Knight of the Trapezoid. Normally the Order is only open to those who have reached the grade of Adept in the Temple of Set, but apparently due to my extensive previous work in the field of Germanic esotericism (both practical and academic)— an exception was made. This was, I think, the result of my open approach to the Temple and to the Order. I let loose with a barrage of material, manuscripts, bibliographies, working reports, and so on. I held nothing back, and my work, given its acceptance and effectiveness in the objective universe was likewise evaluated in a positive way by the Temple and the Order. I owe a debt of gratitude to Betty Ford and Michael Aquino, who at the time was both Grand Master of the Order of the Trapezoid and the High Priest of the Temple of Set, for their generous reception of me and my work in the Temple. I might also add that as soon as I saw that the Order of the Trapezoid was the gate, and that the O.S.T. would only be an unNecessary complication— I officially disbanded it at once and informed the Temple of my action.

Although it would be until the end of the next year before my first actual article ("Mysteries of the Graal") would appear in the official organ of the Order, *Runes*, I was constantly amazed that material that I would send to the Grand Master, Michael Aquino, intending it only as personal correspondence, would show up as published material in the journal.

On June 4, 1984, I was Recognized as an Adept in the Temple of Set— based I am told on the quality of my magical and academic work (which included several manuscripts and one published book). It was a day of pride for me, which only added to the impetus I had gotten a few weeks earlier when I had the degree of Doctor of Philosophy conferred upon me by the University of Texas at Austin.

On October 7 of that same year, I was Recognized to the Priesthood of Set and as a Master of the Order of the Trapezoid during a Working which linked Austin, Texas with ritual events taking place at the Set-V Conclave in Santa Cruz, California. This was done by means of a speaker-phone linkage— just one of the early manifestations of the *Magia Technica* to come.

It was from this time forward that I began to make regular and extensive contributions to the Order's journal, *Runes*. By May of 1986 I had become editor of *Runes*, and so my input into the journal became even more conspicuous. During the years 1986 to 1988, especially, *Runes* became a Workshop for my efforts

On January 18, 1987 I was Recognized to the Grand Mastery of the Order of the Trapezoid, as Michael Aquino assumed the title of Grand Master Emeritus. By the way, this office has nothing to do with the High Priesthood of Set, or the administration of the Temple.

This present book is called *Black Rûna*. This name refers to two things: the word "Black" refers to the Left-Hand Path character of the Work contained herein, but the word "Rûna" is a reference to the Word RÛNA, which was Uttered by me on December 20 (Mother Night) 1988. The Utterance was finally officially Recognized by the Temple of Set on July 13, 1990.

This book gives some deep-background on the character of the Word RÛNA from several different angles. In essence the Word means: "A Sense of the Hidden," and is the Arcanic Principle implicit in the core depth of the sentient Self and in the outermost reaches beyond the limits of the cosmos. RÛNA is the sense of the mysterious that drives us toward inquiry and discovery of the unknown. But the principle itself can never be fully uncovered, because it is the principle of the *Hidden* itself. It is the Darkness which leads to the Light. I have been through the Darkness, to bring forth this Light. Do not turn away from it because it appears to glow with an eerie luminescence, for such is the kind of light by which the first Runes were beheld by the one Eye of Woden.

II

The works presented in this collection were originally written in the context of the Initiatory philosophy of the Temple of Set. In order for readers unfamiliar with this philosophical context to understand the contents more precisely, certain terms must be defined and a true context established. The potential for confusion is great— but so is the possibility for understanding.

This work as a whole has been offered to the world, on a limited basis, in the hopes of developing a greater understanding for the *truth* of the Left-Hand Path.

Much of the following with regard to definitions of technical terms has been adapted from my 1993 manuscript entitled *Lords of the Left-Hand Path: A History of Spiritual Dissent*, a third edition of which was eventually widely published by Inner Traditions (2012).

Before one can embark on a path or a way, one must orient one's self in the universe. The universe is the totality of existence both known and unknown. This is a complex model, divided into at least two components: 1) the objective universe and 2) the subjective universe. The objective universe is the natural cosmos— or world order. This is essentially mechanical or organic, i.e. it is ruled by certain predictable laws manifested in a time/space continuum. The objective universe, including the laws governing it, can be equated with "nature" as well as with "God" in the Judeo-Christian tradition. All of natural science as well as orthodox theology is predicated on the concept that these laws of the objective universe can be discovered and quantified or described in a purely rational manner in the first instance or by "divine revelation" in the other. When considered closely it is evident that what is usually referred to as "God" in orthodox religions is actually identical to that which he is said to create— the natural /mechanical /organic order— or cosmos. It might also be pointed out that there has generally been a popular but sometimes misleading distinction between the concepts "mechanical" and "organic." On one level they are the same in that both are governed by predictable laws. A clock-work or the human body are both ruled and maintained by certain mechanical structures which allow them to function in their environments. At another level there is a distinction between the mechanical and the organic in that the organic model has the ability to propagate and mutate its mechanical structures to ensure its survival. This is possible because there are coded mechanisms within the organism expressly for this purpose (DNA) and because the malleable molecular structure of the mechanism allows for these mutations.

The subjective universe is the "world" of any sentient entity within the universe. There are as many subjective universes as there are sentient beings. The subjective universe is the particularized manifestation of consciousness within the universe. Usually experience of the objective universe is only indirect as information concerning it must come through the subjective universe. Curiously enough the subjective universe does not seem governed by the same natural/mechanical/organic laws as the objective universe— in fact this is the main distinction between them. The subjective universe has the option of acting in a non-natural way, i.e. free from the limitations of the world of five senses and three dimensions.

At this point it might be worth pointing out that the terms objective/subjective have nothing in common with the distinction between accurate/inaccurate, or exact/inexact which popular usage might have projected onto the terms. The subjective universe is capable of far more accurate and exact manifold operations than the objective universe— your reading and understanding of these words is based on the exercise of a faculty within your subjective universe. In simple grammatical terms the subject is the reader, i.e. that which reads, and the object is that which is read. The subjective universe is capable of a full spectrum of possibilities which range from virtually absolute precisions to almost total delusion because it is not bound by natural laws. The focus or epicenter of this non-natural subjective universe is equated with human consciousness, or soul, or self.

The non-natural aspect of this soul is clearly and basically indicated by humanity's drive to impose structures artificially created in that subjective universe upon the objective universe. All artificially created structures (i.e. those made by art/craft) are by definition something separate and apart from the natural cosmos— be those structures pyramids, poems, or political institutions. Animals, many of which may have complex social organizations, are bound by nature and by their organic programming. The wolf-pack, no matter if in one part of the world or another, now or a million years ago, has the same social order. But you will look in vain to find any two human social institutions that are absolutely identical. Anything which is the product of the subjective universe — individual or collective — will bear the mark of variation.

Each particular instance of this soul — this phenomenon of the subjective universe — implies the existence of a first form or general principle from which all the particular manifestations are derived. In the most philosophically refined of the schools of the Left-Hand Path this first principle of isolate intelligence is identified as the "Prince of Darkness"— the ultimate deity of the Left-Hand Path. In the Temple of Set, the initiatory framework in which the documents printed in this collection were created, this Principle is often identified with the Egyptian God Set. But to be more precise, this is the archetype of Selfhood from which all particular and individual selves are derived. This is also an element of the non-natural universe which objectively belongs to the universe itself. In this way the Prince of Darkness can be seen as an independent sentient being in the universe because this is the very principle of that quality in the universe. Humanity is the only species we know of which shares that quality.

The central question now becomes what is the way in which this conscious, free soul is going to relate to, or seek to interact with, the objective universe or the universe as a whole. The Right-Hand Path answers this question simply by saying that the subjective universe must harmonize itself with the laws of the objective universe— be that envisioned as God or nature. Humanity is to seek knowledge of the law, and then apply itself to submitting to that law in order to gain ultimate union with the objective universe, with God, or nature. The Right-Hand Path is the path of union with universal reality (God or Nature). When this union is completed the individual self will be annihilated, the individual will become one with the divine or natural cosmic order. In this state the ego is destroyed as "heaven" is entered or a nirvanic existence/non-existence is "attained." This is clearly the goal of all orthodox Judaic/Christian/Islamic or Buddhistic sects.

The Left-Hand Path considers the position of humanity as it is; it takes into account the manifest and deep-seated desire of each human being to be a free, empowered, independent actor within his or her world. The pleasure and pain made possible by independent existence are seen as something to be embraced and as the most reasonable signs of the highest, most noble destiny possible for humans to attain— a kind of independent existence on a level usually thought of as divine.

Just as most humans go through their natural, everyday lives seeking that which will give them maximal amounts of such things as knowledge, power, freedom, independence and distinction within their world, those of us who walk the Left-Hand Path logically extend this to the non-natural realm. We reject Right-Hand Path admonitions that such "spiritual behavior" is "evil" and that we should basically "get with the program" — of God, of Nature, or whatever —and become good "company men." The self-awareness of independence is seen by many as the fundamental reality of the human condition— we can accept it and live, or reject it and die. By accepting the internal, known reality of human consciousness as eternally dynamic — ever moving, ever changing — existence is embraced; by rejecting it and embracing an external, unknown reality of God/Nature, an eternally static— ever still and permanent — existence is accepted. From a certain enlightened perspective, both paths can be perfectly good from a moral perspective, it is just a matter of the conscious exercise of the will to follow one of these paths in an aware state without self-delusion.

Essentially, the Left-Hand Path is then the path of non-union with the objective universe. It is the way of isolating consciousness within the subjective universe and, in a state of self-imposed psychic solitude, refining the soul or psyche to ever more perfect levels. The objective universe is then made to harmonize itself with the will of the individual psyche instead of the other way around. Where the Right-Hand Path is theocentric (or certainly alleocentric— "other-centered"), the Left-Hand Path is psyche-centric, or soul/self-centered. Those within the Left-Hand Path may argue over the nature of this self/ego/soul, but that the individual is the epicenter of the path itself seems undisputed. An eternal separation of the individual intelligence from the objective universe is sought in the Left-Hand Path. This amounts to an immortality of the independent self consciousness moving within the objective universe and interacting with it at will.

The terms "White Magic" and "Black Magic" have been so bandied about in popular jargon that they might be said to have lost most of their meaningfulness. For my purposes I will restore them to a meaningful philosophical context. Magic can be defined as a methodology by which the configuration of the subjective or objective universe is altered through an act of will originating within the psyche, or the core of the individual subjective universe.

There is no one definition of magic universally accepted by academics and practicing magicians alike, nor is there common agreement on the distinctions between religion and magic. But taking most of the current theories into account a more comprehensive definition might be ventured: Magic is the willed application of symbolic methods to cause or prevent changes in the universe by means of symbolic acts of communication with paranormal factors. These factors could be inside or outside the subjective universe of the operator. Magic is a way to make things happen that ordinarily would not happen. Religion may be distinguished from magic only when the nature of the human will is taken into account. In magic the individual will is primary and is considered to have a real and independent existence. The magician makes the universe do his bidding, to harmonize itself with his will, whereas in religion the human community attempts to harmonize its behavior with a universal pattern, be it God or Nature.

In a precise sense the distinction between White and Black Magic is that White Magic is a methodology for the promotion of union with the universe and pursuing aims in harmony with those of the universe, while Black Magic is such a methodology for the exercise of independence from the universe and pursuing self-oriented aims. Structurally, White Magic has much in common with religion as defined above, while Black Magic is more purely magical in and of itself. This is why magic as a category of behavior is often condemned by orthodox religious systems. For the sake of precise understanding White Magic is a designation for the spiritual technology of the Right-Hand Path and Black Magic is such a designation for that of the Left-Hand Path.

To make even more precise what is meant by the Left-Hand Path, I offer two major criteria: A) the effort toward Deification of the Self and B) that of the practice of Antinomianism. The first of these is complex: The system of thought proposed by the magician must be one that promotes individual self-deification, preferably based on an initiatorily magical scheme. This first criterion can be seen to have four distinct elements:
1) Self-deification— attainment of an enlightened (or awakened), independently existing intellect and its relative immortality.
2) Individualism— the enlightened intellect is that of a given individual, not a collective body.
3) Initiation— the enlightenment and strength of essence necessary for the desired state of evolution of self are attained by means of stages created by the will of the magician, not because he or she was "divine" to begin with.
4) Magic— practitioners of the Left-Hand Path see themselves as using their own wills in a rationally intuited system or spiritual technology designed to cause the universe around them to conform to their self-willed patterns.

The second major criterion, Antinomianism, states that practitioners think of themselves as "going against the grain" of their culturally conditioned and conventional norms of "good" and "evil." True practitioners of the Left-Hand Path will have the spiritual courage to identify themselves with the cultural norms of "evil." There will be an embracing of the symbols of conventional "evil," or "impurity," or "rationality," or whatever quality the conventional culture fears and loathes. Practitioners of the Left-Hand Path will set themselves apart from their fellow humans, will actually or figuratively become outsiders, in order to gain the kind of inner independence necessary for the other initiatory work present in the first criterion. The practice of this second criterion often manifests itself in "antinomianism," that is, the purposeful reversal of conventional normatives: "evil" becomes "good," "impure" becomes "pure," "darkness" becomes "light."

Literally antinomianism implies something "against the law." But the practitioner of the Left-Hand Path is not a criminal in the usual sense. He or she is bound to break the cosmic laws of nature and to break the conventional social laws imposed by ignorance and intolerance. But in so doing the Left-Hand Path practitioner seeks a "higher law" of reality founded on knowledge and power. Although beyond good and evil, this path requires the most rigorous of ethical standards. These standards are based on understanding and not on blind obedience to external authorities.

This latter characteristic of the true Left-Hand Path is the chief cause of its misunderstanding, not only for those on the outside, but for some who would follow this path as well. It takes an enormous amount of spiritual courage to persevere in the face of rejection by not only the world around us but by elements within our own subjective universes as well. Many break under the strain and fall away from the aim and sink back into the morass of cultural norms.

In summary, to be a practitioner of the Left-Hand Path, one must at some point reject the forms of conventional "good" and embraced those of conventional "evil," and have practiced antinomianism, as part of the effort to gain a permanent, independent, enlightened and empowered level of being. This self-deification is not sufficient without this "Satanic" (i.e. "antinomian") component which acts as a guide through the quagmire of popular sentiment and conventional beliefs.

To my personal way of thinking today, the philosophy of the Order of the Trapezoid and the Temple of Set need not be described as "Satanic." However, for initiation on the Left-Hand Path to be effective for those who have just begun the Work on that path, the *antinomian* aspect of the Work does Need to be fulfilled by some means. This antinomianism is the only real reason to make use of Satanic imagery at all— and recent history has shown that this imagery, along with that connected to National Socialism, is still unmatched as a way to arouse the sense of the taboo and forbidden in our culture. This is the indispensable usefulness of this imagery, and this is the root of our interest in things of a "diabolical" character.

The study of the political phenomenon of German National Socialism (1933-1945) has drawn considerable attention to the Order in the past. Interest in this phenomenon is entirely theoretical and structural — and *Magical* — and has nothing whatsoever to do with the racial dogmas of the Nazis. The Order of the Trapezoid has Knights and Dames of a myriad of racial and religious backgrounds. But it must be conceded that the *imagery* does hold an awesome *power* that many do not suspect— more than once we have seen Initiates "spin out" and lose control of themselves and their own Initiations due to the volatile power of some of the symbols and technologies with which we Work.

In case you hadn't heard, and contrary to what most modern-day peddlers of "occult philosophies" try to tell you— *magic* is not easy, it is the hardest thing for humans to do well. Moreover, Black Magic is not only difficult, it is also *dangerous*. It is dangerous precisely because it works with such powerful ideas so directly. Great and difficult tasks call for strong measures. But this strength must be applied with the greatest precision and the highest understanding, or the Black Magician can end up like Humpty-Dumpty.

III

The Order of the Trapezoid is a magical concept, a magical body that exists beyond the limitations of time and space. For example, it was darkly perceived in the dream-scapes of the American fantasy and science fiction writer, H.P. Lovecraft, who wrote of an Order of the Shining Trapezohedron in his tale "Haunter of the Dark." Anton LaVey conceived of the Order of the Trapezoid as the secret core of his Church of Satan. In 1983, or in the Year XVIII by our internal reckoning, Michael Aquino reconstituted the Order as a Working Order of Chivalry as a result of his now famous Wewelsburg Working on October 19, 1982. This Working was conducted in the Hall of the Slain, or Walhalla, of the Wewelsburg, a castle used by Heinrich Himmler as the magical headquarters of his own "Black Order."

In the Charter of the Order of the Trapezoid, issued by Michael Aquino on January 30, 1983, the Grand Master defined the Order thusly:

> The Order of the Trapezoid is an order of knighthood characterized by strict personal honor and faithfulness to the quest for the Grail. The O.Tr. is a *knighthood* in that its members are pledged to traditional chivalric virtues as appropriate to each situation encountered. By *honor* is meant a sense of justice, ethics, and responsibility prior to personal comfort, convenience, or advantage. This honor is known by one's *faithfulness* to the Quest for the Grail, which is the self, soul or psyche made perfect through conscious refinement and exercise of the Will. Attainment of the Grail results in transformation of the individual into a state of dynamic existence energized by the psyche, not by the physical body derived from the material universe. Hence the O.Tr. is the gate to psychecentric immortality beyond physical death.

For whomsoever understands these words a gate shall be opened.

IV

A few words must also be said in conclusion about the editing of the manuscripts of the articles which appear in the following pages. They have all been revised only in minimal details from their form as they first appeared in the pages of *Runes*, the internal organ of the Order of the Trapezoid. Revisions have been for the sake of clarity or usage. Additional information being added in 1995 appears for the most part in square brackets [...] or in notes appearing as "Commentary" after some of the articles. Information in parentheses was so placed in the original work. The articles are presented here in the order they were published, without regard to subject matter.

It should be noted also that this does *not* represent my total production for publication in the pages of *Runes* for the years covered. Contributions of a ritual or

Working dimension have been omitted as reserved for intra-member distribution only, as have other writings of an Initiatory or administrative character. Neither have works been presented here which were studies later published in book form. These would include studies of the *Fraternitas Saturni* (*Runes* Volume V:6 [1987] and VI:1 [1988], which were used in *Fire and Ice*, 1990), "The Runic Spring" (*Runes* VI:5 [1988], published in *Rune Might*, 1990) and "Operative Hexology" (*Runes* VIII:2 [1990], published in *Northern Magic*, 1992).

                                              Stephen Edred Flowers ᛏ
                                              Woodharrow
                                              January 30, XXX (1995ce)

MYSTERIES OF THE GRAAL
(Runes III:5 1985)

A curious mystery recently came to my attention while I was perusing some scholarly journals. In an article entitled "Wolfram's *calix lapideus*" by H.-W. Schäfer the author claims to have found the Graal! He identifies Wolfram's Graal with a certain stone chalice now found in the Cathedral of Valencia, Spain. His reason for doing so is the strange "Arabic" inscription found on the bottom of the object. The inscription appears:

...and is transliterated as "ALABSIT SILIS." Schäfer identifies this with the phrase *lapisit exilis* (Latin: *lapsit exillis*) that occurs in Book IX, section 469 of Wolfram von Eschenbach's epic poem *Parzivâl*. Thus he identifies the *stone* with the stone chalice. So far, it might seem, a plausible assumption. But is this really the Graal itself? And if it is — or even if it is not — what is the significance of the inscription?

In a footnote Schäfer reports a curious fact— one that no doubt would raise an eyebrow of Dr. I. Jones. In trying to convince the reader that the chalice is Wolfram's Graal, Schäfer indicates that at one point (Book IX, Section 471) Wolfram says that the Graal was brought to Earth by angels, and that this chalice of Valencia originally had a base upon which four angels were carved. But then, in an aside within the footnote, he tells us that base was "lost" in *1936*! Now we need not give much of a history lesson to show *who* — from 1933 to 1945 — might have been responsible for the "disappearance" of certain objects in lands over which they had total or partial control!

It is my speculative hypothesis that the Graal-stone is not the chalice, but an object hidden within the base. This idea had occurred to me long before I read this article. The base upon which the chalice stands is the *true* Graal: the chalice may even be a sort of "decoy" object. But those who know — the *Wissenden* — are not fooled by the chalice, which is symbolic of the Graal force but not an actual expression of it. Wolfram was not duped — and, apparently, neither were those responsible for the disappearance of the base of the Valencia "graal." [Whether this base *actually* contains or contained the Graal-stone is one question; whether those who took it *believed* this to be the case is another.]

Now what about the inscription? It seems that Schäfer is correct in his epigraphical analysis; the inscription probably does represent *lapisit exil(l)is*. This could refer to several things: (1) the stone chalice itself, (2) something that was near [in or under] the chalice, or (3) something completely "other" [of which the chalice was a symbol]. The first possibility is favored by Schäfer. We would favor the second. Concerning the third, it is a decided possibility — given the Arabic cultural context of the inscription — that the inscription refers to the "philosophers' stone." The fact that an alchemical term would be translated into Latin, and then transliterated into Arabic script seems strange, but Moorish Spain *was* a strange place.

Actually it is quite plausible to combine possibilities two and three and say that the hidden stone in the base and the "philosophers' stone" are one and the same. This is the solution I ultimately favor, mainly because it corroborates an illuminative Working in which I envisioned the Graal-stone:

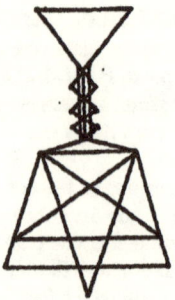

Here the chalice is symbolic of the way in which the trapezohedron actually *works* on consciousness. The chalice symbolizes something from which *Essential* nourishment — and ecstasy — are obtained. In addition, its standard shape indicates a spiral vortex of energy. But whereas the chalice properly *symbolizes* these things, the trapezoid can actually *do* them. It might be said that *any* trapezoid is the *true Graal*— because the power is in the *shape*, not in the substance. However, it is very probable, based on my speculations coupled with historical patterns, that *the* famous Graal-stone upon which the Wolfram/Kyôt tradition is based is/was a lump of meteoric substance cut and polished into a trapezohedron.

This could have been used as a "shew stone" — much like that of Dr. John Dee's black obsidian mirror(s) — ultimately of Meso-American origin. [It is unclear whether Dee had more than one of these black obsidian mirrors. The one preserved in the British Museum is round. In a contemporary illustration, however, Dee is shown with a trapezoidal, or at least angular one. Were there *two*, or is the illustration inaccurate?]

The visions obtained through such a Graal shew-stone could be spoken of metaphorically as the "heathen script" that is "read" by the Graal-Knights. The whereabouts of the stone are unknown.

If my analyses are correct, the *true* Graal has been found in the shape and effects of the trapezoid. This is the knowledge borne within the Order of the Trapezoid. *If* any such stone as referred to in the Wolfram/Kyôt tradition ever actually existed, its discovery and/or recovery would probably be a disappointment the non-initiate, who would not be able to "read the heathen script" or gain Essential nourishment from it. The initiate would find such a discovery a delightful thing, but perhaps only as a fine and rare example of one of his working tools. The power is in the way consciousness interacts with form, not in the thing or substance itself. But there *may* be more to *this* particular substance than we know right now . . .

ON THE WAY OF WOTAN AND THE LEFT-HAND PATH
(*Runes* III:5 1985)

The first principle of the Left-Hand Path is *non-union* — or, more correctly and positively: continuing, (dynamic) independent evolution. This is the meaning of Walhalla.

This principle of the Left-Hand Path is opposed by the Right-Hand Path which dictates *union* — i.e. terminal (static) dependent non-evolution. The followers of the Right-Hand Path seek servitude and eventual absorption by the thing they call God. This is not the time or place to delineate *what* the Right-Hand Path truly is. [It is so confused that even its own followers are often unsure of its nature.] What we want to show here is the Essential Left-Hand Path character of the Way of Wotan, characterized by the teaching of Walhalla.

One of the simplest ways to determine whether a path is of the Right-Hand or of the Left-Hand is to examine the presumed final destination of an adherent's soul or Essence. This is where the confusion of the Christian Right-Hand Path is most conspicuous. On the one hand (pun intended) they desire *union with*, and servitude to, their deity. On the other hand — and on a deep-seated, perhaps genetic level — they desire *ego survival* "in heaven." But what are they to *do* with their immortal egos? What is their purpose? No *orthodox* answer gets us much beyond harp-strumming (= inactivity, stasis). The Left-Hand Path is characterized by *activity* and *purpose* — in this life and in any that is to come.

The Odian path — or the Way of Wotan — - of the ancient Germans is the only historical example of a *national* school of the Left-Hand Path. To simplify, without being inaccurate, the ancient Germanic peoples believed in three possible destinations for the souls of the dead: (1) Hel, (2) back to Midhgardhr (through "rebirth"), and (3) Walhalla (Old Norse *Valhöll*). In Hel they "live" in a static state, being slowly reabsorbed into the cosmo-organic mechanism of Yggdrasill. Hel, which simply means "the enclosed hidden place (of death)," is the normal destination for the vast majority of humanity. The Erulians, those on the path of becoming — signified by the shining power of the Æsir from whom they are descended — reside only temporarily in Hel, after which they are reborn into Middle Earth, the world of humans. *Only* there can they carry on certain Works and continue to evolve. The majority of those reborn wish to continue to be reborn in Middle Earth, as this path is generally considered to be a good thing. After a cycle of such rebirths, the refined and empowered Self of the Erulian, each unique and recognizable, enters into Walhalla within the walls of Asgardhr to become part of the *Einherjar*. Wotan's cosmic army. No "dogma" has ever been developed about specific numbers of cycles, etc. That would definitely detract from the idea of each individual's experience being unique.

Existence in Walhalla is of a threefold character: (1) It is above all *active*, constant endeavor of one kind or another. (2) It is *pleasurable*, usually being described as feasting and entertainment in the hall. (3) It has *great purpose* as preparation for the "final conflict" in which the world will be transformed and renewed.

In the teaching of Walhalla we recognize the Essence of the Left-Hand Path. The heroes who dwell there are immortal and unique, individual participants in a process of evolution of which both they and the cosmos partake. They are *active* agents in this process of Becoming.

Perhaps the most important aspect of the Way of Wotan is the Odian's relationship with the god Óðinn (Wotan). The Odian Left-Hand Path does not seek union with Óðinn: Óðinn is complete unto himself and in his manifold Essence. Rather, Óðinn is an exemplary model to his men and women. He shows them the Ways (complex and hardly monolithic patterns of Working) to acquire an Essential character of transformational, synthetic consciousness as he in fact has done. For his cosmic aims to be attained — and they are by no means assured — he has a vested interest in cultivating unique, innovative souls into his army, the *Einherjar*. The very name *Einherjar* really tells the whole story. The prefix *ein-* means the *singular*— the unique, the "one and only." *Herjar* is the plural of *heri*: "warrior." Each entity in Wotan's host of demi-gods is singular and unique— a band of Óðinn –like being, whose purpose is to guide events in the cosmos and to ensure its continued evolution towards ever more perfect forms.

It would be misleading to leave the reader with the impression that "this life" is considered only a preparation for induction into a "celestial" host. The teaching of rebirth shows the *central* importance of existence in Midgard, the crucible of transformation. Nevertheless this examination of the ultimate destiny of the Erulian soul certainly clarifies the Essential Left-Hand nature of the Way of Wotan by a crystalline method.

As a postscript, it is interesting to note the virtual mock nature of the conflict in the Germanic (Erulian) mythos. Hel and Walhalla cooperate in the evolution of the cosmos, each with its unique mission. In the "final" conflict between the forces of Asgardhr/Walhalla and those of Utgardhr (= Hel/Jötunheimr/Muspellsheimr), Óðinn actually turns to face himself and his own darker creations (= shapings) in Loki and the Fenris-Wolf. The view of Ragnarök as a transformational Working will have to wait until another time. But compare this Left-Hand Path viewpoint to that of the Right-Hand Judeo-Christian mythos, characterized by fear, misunderstanding, and panic— all of which lead to total destruction and to ultimate, universal stasis.

[For a more in-depth study of the god-form of Wotan, see my book *Wodhanaz*.]

THE COMMAND TO LOOK
(*Runes* IV:3 1986)

In the Charter of the Order of the Trapezoid I read that one of Anton LaVey's primal source works for the principles underlying the Law of the Trapezoid and hence the Order itself, was a book by William Mortensen: *The Command to Look*. I had never seen nor heard of this book before, so I set out to find it. I was on the track of the Trapezoid— which is sometimes an elusive trail. As I began looking, I soon discovered that *The Command to Look* was no arcane Black Book, but appeared in the University of Texas card catalog as a book on photographic techniques. My interest waned slightly. Besides, the only copy was in the Humanities Research Center which is also home to much of Aleister Crowley's personal library. That always means red tape. I put off my quest for a few weeks.

Weeks turned into months before I moved myself to take up the trail again. After finding the right collection on the right floor, and after sitting through the required slide show on how to handle rare items in the collection. After the librarian asked "Are you sure you want to do this?"— I knew I was on to something.

I was shown to a private reading room where I finally got the book — presumably dug out of some unseen vault. It was laid before me in a plexiglass "cradle" which is to prevent damage to the tome. What did I see? There on the cover of a small book I was confronted by the face of a baby who looked like a refugee from a Norman Rockwell painting. The librarian sarcastically remarked, "Looks *real* interesting..."

Since I had gone that far, I opened the book, I did not now expect much. But I was very much surprised. *The Command to Look* is indeed a treasure trove of the Black Art, and the ideas contained in it should be made available to the Order not only on historical grounds, but also on the basis of their practical magical value.

Theory

Mortensen insists that the main premise of the Command to Look (CTL) is closer to pure *showmanship* than anything else. The formula is three-fold:

(1) The picture must, by its mere arrangement, make you look at it (IMPACT)
(2) and having looked— *see!* (SUBJECT INTEREST)
(3) and having seen— *enjoy!* (PARTICIPATION)

All three of these elements must be fully activated before the artist — or magician — can be said to have successfully "commanded to look." All three, however, work in such rapid succession that it is almost always effected unconsciously with regard to the viewer— and therefore the artist must carefully formulate his images to work efficiently in all three elements.

The first element — IMPACT — is psychically coercive, and its function is entirely one of the shapes or patterns the viewer sees. It *forces* the viewer to pay attention to the image. This initial force, which Mortensen calls "the pictorial imperative," is the force necessary to overcome the natural inertia of attention which holds most humans in a more or less constant grip. According to Mortensen, IMPACT is purely biological in effect. It is primarily dependent on shapes or patterns that serve as stimuli signaling DANGER. These fear-arousing patterns must have their psychic models stored in the forms within the "racial memory," or to use the Jungian term, "collective unconscious" of humanity.

Mortensen identifies four basic types of pictorial patterns that have the ability to cause this reaction:

1. The DIAGONAL, e.g. the lightning bolt = something that moves *swiftly* with determination
2. The S-CURVE, e.g. the snake (something that approaches in a *slithering* fashion) or the curves of the body (especially female = "the line of beauty")
3. TRIANGLE combinations, e.g. a blade, sharp points or teeth
   (= the threat of *sharpness*)
4. Compact DOMINANT MASS, e.g. large animal or trapezoid
   (= massive block in one's path)

Again it cannot be overemphasized that these patterns are purely *formal* and have nothing to do with the dominant themes of the images. For example, if one drew the outlines of the basic contrasts in a black and white photograph and examined them in a purely geometrical way, the "pictorial pattern" would be obvious. More than one category of pictorial patterning can be present in any given representation as well.

The second element — SUBJECT INTEREST — must now be able to "deliver" what the successful application of the pictorial imperative has promised. Many images, or magicians, may command to look, and then be quite unable to hold the attention they have attracted. This is done through the actual subject of the image, moving from the external form to the internal essence of the thing. According to Mortensen, in order to hold the attention — in order to make the viewer *see* — he or she must at once be able to *recognize* something basically and essentially compelling about the subject. For all practical purposes, this *recognition*, must occur simultaneously with the IMPACT. Therefore, the types of SUBJECT INTERESTS must have as broad an emotional appeal as possible. Mortensen cites the great showman, Cecil B. De Mille, as saying that the formula for box office success is to have a film dealing with sex, sentiment, religion, and sport. Mortensen reduces this somewhat to three subject themes:

    1. SEX
    2. SENTIMENT
    3. WONDER

It is Mortensen's contention that their compelling nature make them the most effective imagematic themes in the CTL.

The sex-theme seems to dominate — it certainly does in Mortensen's own work. In commenting on the gender of the subject of the sex-theme image, Mortensen says: "It is interesting to note that women are just as much attracted to the theme of sex when presented in the form of the female nude as men are. Their attraction in this case is vicarious, rather than direct. Their pleasure comes in *imagining* themselves placed in a situation where they would receive the same admiration that goes out to the theme of the picture." (p. 37).

The sentiment-theme is usually effected through the softer aspects of sex; children, hardships of humble life, domestic life, animals, landscapes, national pride, glamour of the past, etc.

The wonder-theme is quite broad and covers the areas of unknown, uncertain, mysterious things, as well as themes of the supernatural, the macabre, etc.

Themes can, of course, be effectively mixed. Some permutations, such as sex + wonder might be more immediately effective than sex + sentiment, but as with all forms of communication, it would seem that knowledge of one's potential "target audience" is the essential variable.

It should be obvious that the effective use of the CTL is largely dependent upon the æsthetic compatibility of the nature of the IMPACT pattern and SUBJECT matter. Interesting mixtures are also possible here.

The third element of the CTL-formula is PARTICIPATION, the element that causes the looker *to experience* — and thereby enjoy — what he or she is seeing. This is done, according to Mortensen, by drawing the viewer's attention into the image by means of lines — geometrical alignments — that cause a movement of those attention patterns in accordance with the IMPACT and SUBJECT matter of the image. Mortensen comments that the eye of the looker will naturally move along contours and outlines, and that such geometrical guides should be provided by the image-maker in ways compatible with the IMPACT lines and the SUBJECT matter. This is what he would call "confirming forms." The image-maker must, with this third element, confirm the promised subject matter after having "commanded to look" in the first place with an almost pure "shock element."

Practice

There are at least three ways to apply the principles of the CTL—
1) in the creation of graphic or spatial images (e.g. photographs, drawings, paintings rooms, chambers, etc.), 2) in Lesser Black Magic, and 3) in Greater Black Magic.

The first application is obvious and primarily what Mortensen had in mind. The work of Edward T. Hall, e.g. *The Hidden Dimension*, is a valuable supplement to the CTL in this regard. Of course, the design of a Trapezoidal Working Chamber could not ignore these principles either.

In reading Mortensen's book, the Black Magician probably could not escape the feeling that these principles could be applied outside the context of the graphic or spatial arts. If indeed these principles are "biological" or part of the "racial memory," could they not be employed when the Black Magician considers how to present himself or herself when working Lesser Black Magic? It seems that the CTL contains a comprehensive theory on how to get — and hold — the attention of someone on an unconscious level. What, then, the Black magician does with that attention is another matter. However, it is clear that when one looks around that CTL is being employed by a variety of individuals, both consciously and unconsciously, all the time.

Finally, the CTL can be used in Greater Black Magic. The Black Magician can use its principles to impress more effective images within the subjective universe and thereby have a greater or deeper effect in the objective universe. Also, any objective manifestation of this process — in an objective image constructed according to CTL principles — will be a more powerful tool in effecting Greater Black Magic. This is where the Law of the Trapezoid comes in. If we analyze the

Seal of the Order[‡] we will see a (Grand) Masterful application of CTL principles: the "swiftly moving diagonal" its center (the head of the *tcham*-scepter), the "threat of sharpness" throughout (not especially the interlockings of the numerals with the angles of the pentagram and the –w– at its nether point), and the "dominant mass" implicit in the trapezoid itself.

The Black magical applications of the CTL seem virtually boundless, and it is to the credit of Anton Szandor LaVey, first Grand Master of the Order of the Trapezoid, and perhaps the greatest magical genius of this century, that he was first able to extract the practical magical applications from Mortensen's æsthetic theories.

Postscript

When I returned to the H.R.C. for a second time to read the Mortensen text in preparation for this article, I found that those in the library who had formerly been so sarcastic about the book were now well acquainted with what they called "that weird book." In fact, I found that it had not been returned to "the vault" since my first visit, and it had become quite a sensation among the staff.

[2019: *The Command to Look* was published in a new edition in 2014 by Feral House with an important forty-three page essay on the importance of the book entitled "Infernal Impact: The Command to Look as a Formula for Satanic Success" by Michael Moynihan.]

[‡] Michael Aquino, "Evolution of the Order of the Trapezoid Insignia" *Runes* IV:2, pp. 11-16.

TRAPEZOIDAL RUNOLOGY
(*Runes* IV:4 1986)

According to my own understanding of the Order of the Trapezoid, it is the more fully evolved manifestation of the true and timeless core of elder Odianism— the complex of ultimate principles at the root of the historical cult of Odin/Wotan. The Wotanic Principle itself is embodied in the A-Rune. There is a clear distinction between what the Order of the Trapezoid *is* and a revival of old pagan practices or levels of understanding. The Order of the Trapezoid *is* and *is becoming* something quite new, but it is based on timeless principles, a complex of dynamic possibilities existing synchronically, which the old Erulians (ancient Odians) first perceived and worked into the runic system. It follows then that the historical runic tradition can be used to help us understand the Principles now emerging in the Trapezoid. But this is definitely not a case of "plugging in" runic values. As Trapezoidal developments might be seen to complete emerging older runic concepts as the older runic values illuminate the more obscure angles of the Trapezoid. I would guess this is because they ontologically meet in that zone of "dynamic possibilities existing synchronically" (*Ginnungagap*).

The uses made of the Runes within the Order are not necessarily the traditional ones made in ancient times by elder Erulian magicians of the North. Our Order seeks to go beyond this into a "runology of the future," which is in perfect harmony with the "spirit" of the elder ones, but by Necessity this "futuristic" runology should be able to incorporate Trapezoidal Principles. It will grow in the minds of all Knights and Dames of the Order who take it up— and in each it will bear forth unique and rare grains of power and wisdom.

What follows is a tentative effort to synthesize runic and Trapezoidal Principles based on this understanding. It is hoped that this will encourage others, especially Knights and Dames of the Order, to expand our common understanding of the system in the glow of the Black Flame.

In these tables, the runic shape, numerical value, phonetic value, Proto-Germanic name and translation / interpretation, and a modern derivative or name of convenience are presented, followed by a short discussion of its Principles.

ᚠ 1. F
fehu, cattle, livestock, money, gold (mobile wealth)
FEE

Principle: Fiery dynamism underlying the origins of all living evolving things. It is the Primal Red Flame [= Life-Force]. The power of magical enthusiasm. The sign of the Rhine-Gold.

ᚢ 2. U
: *uruz*, aurochs; drizzle (vitality)
: UROX

Principle: Vital organic energy of life and original procreation and subsequent transformations. This is the mystery into which the Black Magician links without losing Self in order to Work. Magical Understanding. The Gate which is opened in Working.

ᚦ 3. TH
: *thurisaz*, giant (thurs); *thorn*, thorn (brute force)
: THURS or THORN

Principle: Non-conscious reactive force in the cosmos-- a Thurs. This can be, and must be, wielded by the Black Magician— by the agent of consciousness in the World. The hammer of Thorr — Mjöllnir — outgoing force which can be turned around to form the "Sleep-Thorn" and be used to delve consciously into the unconscious.

ᚨ 4. A
: *ansuz*, the Ase (= Odhinn): sovereign ancestral god of consciousness
: ANS

Principle: Divine consciousness embodied in the human psyche. The Four: the four angles of the Trapezoid. The Principle of psyche-centricism and the process of synthesis. The Divine-Principle. The divine exemplary model. The Magical Word.

ᚱ 5. R
: *raidho*, riding, vehicle
: RIDING

Principle: Rhythmic and proportional dynamism. The Right. The Principle of symmetry and the *phi*-ratio. The functioning, formulaic Principle behind the process of Ritual. The Pentagram— as a demonstration of the *phi*-ratio.

ᚲ 6. K
: *kenaz*, torch (controlled fire)
: KEEN

Principle: Creative fire. The Black Flame of Knowledge— a Principle derived directly from the GIFT (7) within MAN (20). This is the equivalent of the divine fire brought by Prometheus— the spark of inspiration in the creative process.

X 7. G
    gebô, gift, generosity (exchange)
    GIFT
Principle: The GIFT itself: the Gift of Wotan. In Temple terms, the Gift of the Prince of Darkness— the Gift of isolate Intelligence defining the potentially divine Self.] The Form of the Ring (of the Nibelungen) forged within the Self.

P 8. W
    wunjô, joy (ecstasy)
    WYN
Principle: Ideal harmonization of elements in the subjective and objective universes. Subjectively this is experienced as a sort of ecstasy. For the Black Magician this is a means to Willed ends, but for the White Magician it is an end in itself.

H 9. H
    hagalaz, hail(-stone) h [seed-form]
    HAIL
This is the Seed-Principle of all Becoming. The icy hail-stone is a symbol of a transformative substance which enters consciousness from the outside. This is the Graal-Stone. The Mystery of Essence. The Stone from which the Knights and Dames of the Order read the Universal Essence. The insignia of a Master of the Order of the Trapezoid— h.

✝ 10. N
    naudhiz, need (the need-fire)
    NEED
Principle: NEED— resistance or friction in the Universe. It is the impetus which sets in motion the process for the ignition of the Black Flame within the Self of the Black Magician. The Need-Fire is the Self-generated flame that can be impressed on the universal order in Black magical Workings.

| 11. I
   isa, ice (contraction)
   ICE

Principle: Absolute contraction or stasis. This is the darkness of Cosmic Ice (cf. theories of Hans Hörbiger or those concerning "black holes" etc.) This is the zone in which the magical silence and solitude of the Black Magician is cultivated.

♂ 12. J (Y)
   jera, (good-)year (harvest)
   YEAR

Principle: The horizontal [Natural] cycle. This is the Form central to the functioning of mechanical / organic Nature. This is a Form which the Black Magician must learn to understand and to use— without being consumed by it. It provides material rewards for actions undertaken in concert with it.

♂ 13. EI
   eihwaz yew(-column) [verticality]
   YEW or YOGH

Principle: The vertical column. This is the Form central to the workings of non-natural consciousness. The sign of the Spear of Wotan: Gungnir as an expression of the Will of the Black Magician. The Mystery of the World-Tree, Yggdrasill, and the power to traverse various levels of the hypothetical universe.

Ϟ 14. P
   perthro, lot-cup (divinatory tool) [evolutionary essence]
   PERD

Principle: Time. The process of the Three Norns, or Wyrd Sisters, is described in this Rune. It is by this Mystery that the Black Magician can understand the "past" (or the "Ideal") and shape the "future" (or "hypothetical"). The P-Rune is the Trapezohedron as the Well of Mimir— at the nadir of which the Subjective Eye of Wotan is hidden.

ᛉ 15. -Z
:   *elhaz*, elk (nobility)
    ELKS

Principle: The Essential power of the link between the world of Forms and that of Things. The link between the realm of the Trapezoid itself and its Order. The sign of the Graal-Cup. The sign of the valkyries and of the *fylgja* or daimonic Self. The power to receive and wield magical force. The insignia of the Grand Master [and Grand Masters Emeriti]— m.

ᛋ 16. S
:   *sowilo*, sun (crystalline light)
    SUN

Principle: "Higher Being." The ultimate Form to which the Black Magician aspires. It is the goal, and the pathway: when one "SUN" is attained there will always be another... The path of the Lightning Bolt. The power of the Serpent coiled within the Earth and ringing the world from above. The Principle of Honor within the Order. [*Meine Ehre heißt Treue*— My Honor is Known by Faithfulness.]

ᛏ 17. T
:   *teiwaz*, the god Tyr [rationality]
    TIW

Principle: Discipline and the power of logical thought. The Objective Eye of Wotan at the zenith of the Irminsûl. The Principle of Faithfulness [*Treue*] within the Order. The insignia of the Knight and Dame of the Order of the Trapezoid— t.

ᛒ 18. B
:   *berkano*, birch(-goddess) [emergence]
    BIRCH

Principle: Self-contained propagation or growth. The nine angles created by the combination of the Trapezoid (4) with the Pentagram (5).

ᛗ 19. E
> *ehwaz*, (war-)horse [energy]
> EH

Principle: Active and empowered cooperation between *two* entities or elements directed toward definite goals. The "wedding" of MAN (20) and YEW (13)— of the incarnate magician with the Principles of his or her higher [Wode-]Self.

ᛗ 20. M
> *mannaz*, man (= human being)
> MAN

Principle: The incarnate Black Magician as one possessed of the GIFT (7), seeking the higher Existence of the YEW (13). MAN is the essence of the heroic struggle of humanity toward higher Existence beyond death.

ᛚ 21. L
> *laguz*, water (fluidity)
> LAKE

Principle: The Life-Force. The power of Loki in the transformative process and the Essence of the Elixir contained within the Horn or Graal-Cup. [*Becoming*.]

◆ 22. NG
> *ingwaz*, the god Ing [repose]
> ING

Principle: The separation of the evolving Black Magician from the Natural World in a state of non-natural Existence in which Willed Becoming can take place.

ᛞ 23. D
> *dagaz*, day(-light)
> DAY

Principle: The dynamic synthesis of all polar opposites in the central Self of the Black Magician. The light of DAY brings the ultimate state of Magical Awareness and wakefulness. This is the Rune of consciousness enlightened by the Black Flame— the primal Symbol of the Gift of the Prince of Darkness.

ᛝ 24. O
   othala, estate (stationary wealth)
   ODAL
Principle: The complex welding together of diverse entities and elements into a unique form of self-expression. Principle of the Order and of Walhalla.

***+++ ***++++++ *+++++ ***+++ ***+++++++

[Subsequent developments and investigations have demonstrated to me that the *traditional* basis of Runology must be used as the ultimate guide when trying to make use of the Runes. The more *subjective*, and even innovative, approach afforded by Trapezoidal speculation can be valuable as a way to open gateways to new kinds of understanding— but the final test of validity lies in the tradition itself. Beginning with established and objective tradition provides the *precision* that is necessary to guide the *power* generated by subjective enthusiasm to its Willed goals. The advantage to working with a valid, objectively testable, *tradition* is that the Initiate has a transpersonal "touchstone" which can periodically be consulted to determine whether the Initiate is on the right track. This is the true meaning of being able to "read heathen writing" on the facets of the Graal-Stone, or Hail-Stone.]

RUNES AND ANGLES
(Runes IV:4 1986)

It has been noted by German Rune magicians that the Runes are a psychologically engaging script. Each Runic shape fascinates the viewer, as opposed to the flat, lifeless appearance of Roman letters. But what exactly is responsible for this effect? *I think it is to be found to some extent in the Law of the Trapezoid.* If we look at the Latin capitals:

ABCDEFGHIKLMNOPQRSTVXYZ

we will see a predominance of right angles and curves. These right angles tend to lead the eye into "dead ends," and the curves deflect the attention entirely. Now, if we look at the runic futhark:

ᚠᚢᚦᚨᚱᚲᚹ : ᚺᚾᛁᛃᛇᛈᛉᛊ : ᛏᛒᛖᛗᛚᛜᛟᛞ

a different picture emerges. Obtuse and acute angles predominate — with no curves at all. These attract the attention and hold it on the figure or angle itself. There is a possible historical reason for this. Originally the Runes were carved on wood and their shapes were the results of efforts to avoid "going with the grain" and thus losing the distinctive line, a concept with magical import of its own perhaps. But even later, when Runes were written on parchment they kept their unique "obtuse" shapes.

Perhaps this factor is to some extent responsible for the "Command to Look" based purely on the visual impact their shapes also make on the psyche of the viewer. This, coupled with the lore and magical tradition attached to the Runes, only increases this impression— and this reality. The Runes attract attention, hold it, and are able to a large extent to deliver on this initial promise of Mystery and Power.

GRAAL-MYTHOS IN OLD ENGLISH RUNES?
(Runes IV:4 1986)

The ancient Anglo-Saxons expanded the runic futhark to an eventual total of thirty-three runestaves. They were using as many as twenty-nine from the earliest period for which we have records for them (ca. 450 CE). But these were always mere expansions of the twenty-four Rune futhark.

Also from an early time (ca. 700-800 CE) two Runes not belonging to these twenty-nine, Z *calic*: 'chalice' for the "hard" /c/ as in "cup" and , *gâr*: 'spear' for the "hard" /g/ as in "gar," were occasionally being used. For one to two hundred years earlier the related Frisian tradition on the Continent was using additional Rune: } *stân* for /st/. However, in one manuscript — the Cotton MS Domitian A9 of the 11th century — which is probably the clearest, most reliable representation of the codified English tradition in use in the 11th and 12th centuries (ca. 1000-1200 CE) we find these Runes not only present but juxtaposed to one another with their names:

calic   *stân*   *gâr*

I find it more than coincidental that these three elements would be juxtaposed to one another in an ostensibly "secret tradition" at a time and in a place reputed to have been a hot-bed of Grail mysticism. That these are precisely the three elements essential to Wolfram's esoteric vision of the Graal — or one that synthesizes the view of the Graal as chalice and the Graal as stone — seems too much to ignore.

Some may be put off to some extent by what seems to be the Christian symbolism of the Graal— however, the astounding fact is that there is *absolutely nothing Christian about it*. Only *some* of the less enlightened myths of its origins (not that of Wolfram/Kyôt, for example) are Christianized— but these seem late and apologetic. But the actual way in which the Graal and its Order function is precisely un- or counter-Christian, i.e. Christ is not a factor. An early earthly high priest or initiate is chosen from the Order to perform as Graal-King in service of the purely abstract (non-personal) principles represented by the Graal. It is no wonder the whole Graal-Mythos was shunned by the medieval Church.

It seems that the "magical formula" *calic-stân-gâr* actually represents an esoteric understanding of the Graal-Mythos unique to the Germanic world (as far as we know). Although Wolfram refers to southern sources [from Moorish Spain] no hard evidence for this understanding has actually come from there. So we are left with Wolfram's lengthy discourses in *Parzivâl* as well as other discussions in medieval German works, e.g. the *Wartburgkrieg* of Heinrich von Ofterdingen in which the Graal is identified with a stone that fell from Lucifer's crown, and the Old English runic tradition, as sources for the chalice-stone-spear complex. Thus it may well be that this whole complex actually represents a heathen tradition in a heterodox Christian setting. It is not far-fetched to assume that heathen elements would find a safer home in heretical ideas than trying to wedge themselves into orthodox forms (although this also happened).

I think this material is sufficient for any true Black Magician to be able to unravel the significance of the *calic-stân-gâr* complex— perhaps with the one additional piece of information that the spear is certainly *Gungnir*, the spear of Wotan which acts as his scepter of power— the *true* "spear of destiny."

[2019: Although the Christian references to these symbols seems apparent, it may be that there is a deeper set of mythic associations at work in the Arthurian legends. These are explored in the book *From Scythia to Camelot* by Littleton and Malcor which delves into the Iranian connections.]

RUNIC ORIGINS OF THE "PEACE SIGN"
(*Runes* IV:5 1986)

In the early 1960s a curious sign became prevalent which until then had been unknown to most people. It could be seen on buttons, on the sides of micro vans, and often painted or drawn on neighborhood buildings. Perhaps it was first noticed as a sign carried in various left-wing demonstrations for peace and/or nuclear disarmament. It came to be known popularly as the "peace sign."

Among Rune occultists it is popular to assume that anything that is Rune-like is in fact, on some level, actually runic, i.e. mysterious or magical in character. While such forms of ascriptive magical thinking when kept under control can be made meaningful, it might be interesting first to find out whether a given Rune-like sign has factually runic roots. In the case of the "peace sign" this can be shown.

Some years ago I read an account of this sign which was highly unsatisfactory. It stated that the sign was made up of a combination of two letters, N + D, from some obscure alphabet or another, and that these letters stood for "Nuclear Disarmament." Furthermore, it was reported that the sign was first developed and used by British anti-nuclear activists in the early 1960s. [Later I was to discover that the "alphabet" in question was the Semaphore signal system in which ∧ stood for N and ' stood for D. The resulting sign: ⊕ *was* in fact seen in protest groups, but it is distinctly *different* from the more familiar "peace sign."] It seems beyond doubt that the sign was used by such groups at that time, but was it their invention or did they borrow it from some previous source?

As it turns out, the use of this sign was not new to the Left in the 1960s. It had been used, for example, by the anti-Nazi Left in Germany itself and also by clever Russian propagandists on the eastern front. Actually, it is an example of the use of a group's internal symbolism against itself. In the esoteric runology of the early 20th century, chiefly originated by Guido von List and his followers, the sign ⊥ indicated "death." This is in contrast to the sign ⋎ which meant "life." This symbolism quickly spread to popular use in early 20th century Germany, so that even certain newspapers began to print the dates of a person's birth and death prefixed by the signs m and y respectively, e.g. Guido von List ⋎1848 - ⊥1919. Some papers continue the practice to this day. It was well established that these symbols essentially stood for "life" and "death." Perhaps it should be noted that Right Wing organizations have also taken up the "life rune" as a symbol, e.g. on the masthead of the *National Vanguard*.)

The Russians, as the Red Army advanced toward Berlin, distributed leaflets urging the Germans to give up the fight, telling them that the war was lost and that only death awaited them. These leaflets were decorated with the "peace sign" — in this case a sign of death. In the example below, we see a propaganda poster alerting the German Leftists that Heinrich Himmler (i.e. the ᛋᛋ) was to assume responsibility for internal security in Germany as he had done in various lands the Germans had conquered — wherein massive genocide had been practiced. "Now It's OUR Turn!!" the poster declares. Note the use of the "death rune."

It would seem that the sign was later taken up by Leftists. Doubtless, this was due as much to its mysterious allure (common to runic symbols in general) as to its associations with previous causes.

This can be taken as an example of the attraction of signs possessed of the Command to Look (Black Geometry), and also as an example of the use of cultural associations with signs being used in a mode of psychological warfare. It may be a fact that if such signs have their roots in the deep psyche of the group being targeted they will be far more effective than if they are arbitrary and wholly artificial. In this form of Lesser Black Magic, of course, Madison Avenue has far outstripped both Moscow and Berlin.

[*R.I.P.*]

SET AND WOTAN
(*Runes* IV:6 1986)

As an Adept, I conducted a Working on the North Solstice XIX [1984] to help illuminate the relationship between, Woden, the divine Form with which I had Worked for years and the one that had (re-)entered my life in a newly crystalline shape: Set. The result was *The Book of the Wanderings of Woden and Set*. [Available in the Archives of the Order of the Trapezoid and in *The Ruby Tablet of Set*.] But since that Working, I have gained a new perspective — that of a III° Initiate of the Temple. I would like to share some of this new perspective with the readers for at least two reasons. First, it seems important to many Initiates that the relative positions of Wotan and Set within the Order of the Trapezoid be delineated more clearly. Second, such an exposition could act as a prototype for the understanding of other Forms heading Orders within the Temple. Of course, these Forms need not bear an Egyptian æsthetic. For some Initiates this would seem more necessary than for others.

To elucidate this Working further, it is necessary to comment first on the character of the Wotanic Form(s) and then on the Setian Form in order to come to a deeper understanding of the relationship between them.

WOTAN

Here I will concentrate on the Form of Wotan or Woden as conceived in historical epochs of his cult. The application of this Form to that created magically by Richard Wagner in his Ring Cycle would be the subject of another study.

The Form of Woden is that of the questing magical hero. Woden does not constitute the psyche— he *possesses* it. His very name means "Master of Inspiration." But this indicates that he is not the substance of inspiration itself. He acquires this [inspiration or *wôd*] through an initiatory process. Thus he is the heroic archetype [or exemplary model] of The Initiate.

The best example of this is Woden's Runic Initiation in which he hangs for nine nights on the World-Tree Yggdrasill in order to gain access to the runic mysteries. Note: Woden takes up the Runes in already complete [and perfect] Form— he does not "invent" them.

His archetype was spread organically among all those peoples and lands in which Wodenic kings reigned and left their names and blood. These included not only the Germanic lands, but also Russia, Italy, Spain, France and even some areas in North Africa). Woden cannot be "exported" out of certain groups.

As an organic, even "mortal," entity, the Wodenic archetype can, and does, undergo essential change through history. It has apparently learned the secret of turning "death" into the opportunity for metamorphosis. This particular facet is most clearly demonstrated in the myth of Ragnarök in which Woden is swallowed by the Fenris-Wolf. It should be borne in mind that the wolf is one of Woden's own principal "sacred animals." Woden is then avenged by his son Vidharr, who splits open the Wolf, thus implicitly releasing a transformed Woden back into the active world. This rebirth from the Belly of the Beast also survives in the Little Red Riding Hood tale recorded by the Grimms in the early 19th century.

Woden is highly paradoxical. He embodies all extremes in himself and seeks to synthesize all extremes in a comprehensive way. In many regards, the Wodenic Form is an instrument for the synthesis and willed utilization of polarized substances or essences. But ultimately something is missing in this image. Woden is the pure suprarational will to power, knowledge and eternal becoming. [It is also noteworthy that Woden expresses a "will to pleasure"— and that the combination of all these factors lead to the conclusion that we are dealing with a comprehensive Will-to-Life.]‡ But the crystalline Form which makes any coherent expression of these things possible is not inherent in him. In terms of the Germanic ideology this is made possible through the Runes which Woden suprarationally grasps. This comprehension transforms him from a potential god into a true god.

SET

The Form of Set is the crystalline Form of pure Self-Consciousness [or the Principle of Isolate Intelligence]. The Form, although dynamic, is coherent and ordered within itSelf and remains in a perpetual state of separation from the organic/mechanical universe. Ultimately, it should be fairly easy to see why this Form is absolutely necessary to the existence of a Form such as Woden. Without the existence of this Principle, Woden would never be instilled with the suprarational will to seek the hidden (i.e. the Runes: he would never have realized his own isolation. Set, by whatever name, is the prerequisite of all Forms of consciousness and all god-forms for this very reason. This is part of the truth behind the statement found in the *Book of Coming Forth by Night*: "All other gods of all other times and nations have been created by men."

Set is mystifying only in his ultimate simplicity. Once the Form is grasped, other Forms are seen more clearly through its lens, and a new depth of focus is possible.

Without this lens it is impossible to see Self clearly as something separate from other gods, or the mechanism or organism of the universe.

If the ancient Germanic Erulians (i.e. Initiated Rune-Magicians) were to be confronted with the Form of Set — which some may well have been — they would have probably understood that Form in abstract terms— not as a "god" (i.e. an *ansuz*). This Form would certainly be that of the runic system itself. Thus the "Gift of Set" would be the infusion of that Form into the mechanical/organic universe. The role of Woden is that of the archetypal magician who first grasps this Gift and thereby shows the way to his human retinue. Woden also has a Gift— which is the codification of the Runes imparted in the Germano-Runic initiatory system. Thus the ultimate Form is that of "Set," in the Germanic system this Form is a "nameless unknown" abstract [= *Rûna*] as is its counterpart Form HarWer (Horus)— the Form of the "Secrets of the Natural Universe."]. A god, in this case Woden, grasps this Gift and infuses it into man. There is direct mythic evidence for this in the Germanic myth cycles, where the tri-form Woden-Wili-Weh imparts spiritual gifts to the primal man and woman, whom they shape from living vegetable matter (trees), not from dirt! [See the "Völuspá in the *Poetic Edda*, stanzas 17-18.] In ancient times, the special qualities of this Gift were reserved to the Runic Initiates.

It should not seem odd that other gods or goddesses would be involved in the distribution of the Gift of Set. This is the way it seems to have been in Egypt as well. There are few direct references to Set in what most would clearly recognize as a "magical" context— but this Form is presupposed in all acts of consciousness or certainly of true magic. If an ancient Priest of Set were to attempt to understand the Form of Woden completely, he would probably have to make a conglomeration of various gods: Thoth, Anubis, Bes, Osiris, and so on. Beyond this he might see in Woden an expression of the magical conjunction of Set-Horus— under the control of Set but with a benevolent will toward Horus, i.e. toward the organic cosmos.

In the final analysis, Set and Woden have little in common. One Form cannot be mistaken for the other. Rather, these two Forms are complementary. That which we have identified as Set can exist in a void separate from an organic context infused with the Gift. Although it might be incorrect to say that Set precedes Woden in a linearly chronological sense, it is true that Woden presupposes, or even implies, Set [i.e. the Principle of Isolate Intelligence]. This is an important point since it prevents us from assuming that it is only because of Set's chronological or historical *age* that that particular Form is central to the Temple. Actually, it has much more to do with the *quality* of that Form— regardless of its age.

In this regard, something I wrote in a letter (7/12/1987ce) to a modern Odinist seems right to the point:

> The statement in the *Book of Coming Forth by Night* that "all other gods (other than Set) are created by men" is best understood as a statement that it is the power of separate intellectual consciousness imparted by Set which has given mankind the very ability to apprehend the forces and principles of the universe, hence to personify and visualize them as gods. In this sense, Set makes it possible for "Odin" — or Satan — or "YHVH" — or "Cthulhu," for that matter, to exist. Hence I would call the existence and Gift of Set preconditions to the existence of the other gods.

Both of these complementary Forms are to be synthesized in some fashion or another by the psyches of the Knights and Dames of the Order. These two Forms can find their fullest expression only in the psyche of a Working magician. It is there, and only there, that the true relationship between these principles can be understood.

[For a more in-depth study of the god-form Wotan, see my 2018 book *Woðanaz*.]

---

‡ See my article "The Way of Woden" in *Gnosis* 9 (Fall, 1988), pp. 30-35. [This article was subsequently included in the anthology volume *Blue Rûna* (2001).]

WALBURGA IN KHEM
(*Runes* IV:6 1986)

Among all the speculative and magical correlations between *Thule* [Germania] and *Khem* [Egypt] there is one remarkable example that ranks alongside the Sethos II sword (see J. Spanuth, *Atlantis of the North*, p. 42): a copper sword made in northern Europe out of North Sea ore found in 1912 in the Nile delta. This outstanding example is an ostrakon (clay tablet) from Elephantine in far upper Egypt. It is dated from the second century CE and is now housed in the State Museum of Berlin. On this clay tablet there is the name of a Prefect and a list of persons in his retinue. This list includes a certain *Baloubourg Se(m)noni sibylla*, "Waluburg sibyl of the Semnones." The Semnones were a Germanic tribe with their homeland in what is today east central Germany. This is just one piece of evidence of a widespread presence of Germanic people in Egypt during the Roman Age. What makes this one especially interesting is that it shows the presence of Germanic magicians in Egypt, and it identifies one by the name of Walburg.

Walburg may not have been this woman's given name. It is more likely that it was an initiatory or magical name, as it literally means "the stronghold [=-*burg*] of the fallen [= the dead]," and could refer to her otherworldly function as a seeress. By the way, Germanic sibyls were highly trusted in the Mediterranean world, so that it is not surprising that we find such prominent reference to one here. Also, it is interesting to note that the name, which eventually became common as a given name, is the same as we have in St. Walburga, after whom *Walpurgisnacht* ("Walburga's Night") is called. Actually there is some degree of doubt as to whether or not May Eve has anything to do with the historical St. Walburga, a 7th century English abbess. Her festival day is actually in February. It seems more likely that the seeress function was unofficially "canonized" under the name Walburga and celebrated on May Eve in continuation of ancient customs relevant to that time of the year. It can be no accident that the coming forth of the Æon of Satan, and hence that of Set, occurred on just this night.[‡]

Walburga and others like her might very well have been able to learn something of the wisdom of old *Khem* — at that time in a state of being rapidly "democratized" — and to take it back to Germania with them. The great majority of Germanic people in Egypt during the first centuries of the common era were soldiers in the service of Rome. Many of these, once their "tour of duty" was over, returned to their homelands, and probably spread what they had learned among their kinsmen. The Germanic peoples were quite talented at borrowing elements from foreign cultures and adapting them in ways so subtle, that the foreign origins outside Thule were virtually undetectable. The Runes, as a writing system, are one such example.

Not only did the Germans go to Egypt in the first centuries CE, but at the same time Egyptian cults were flourishing in Roman Germany (those border areas along the Rhine and to some especially extent along the Danube colonized by the Romans). There was, of course, an ongoing exchange of people between Roman Germany and Free Germany (where, for example, Walburga, sibyl of the Semnones had her home). The cults of Isis and Serapis were especially active along the Rhine. However, there has never been any evidence for a purely imported cult among the free pagan Germans. The Romans would import cults in a fairly pure state and adopt them into their culture— co-existing more or less with their more native cults. But the free Germans would take a foreign cult as the impetus for innovation within their own indigenous cultic life. They were adaptive, not adoptive.

It may be suspected that the cultural interchange between the Germans and Egyptians in the first four or five centuries of the common era, although not intense, were multileveled. German seeresses probably picked up information from Greco-Egyptian magicians, while German soldiers probably acquired cultic practices from the religion of the military in Egypt, especially that expressed among the foreign military forces. Now, while it might be a bit speculative, the theological context in which the foreign soldier-magician would be most at home in Egypt would be Setian. By this time the notoriously xenophobic Egyptians had long cast Set out into the "foreign rabble," where he/it found safe haven. There his cause could have been secretly nurtured in the heart of darkness to rise again in Form (and eventually in the tenth year of this Æon in name‡) within the European culture— far away in the land of the Hyperboreans.

---

‡ Anton LaVey inaugurated the Church of Satan on Walpurgisnacht, 1966.

TRAPEZOIDAL CINEMA
(*Runes* V:1 1987)

One of the roots of the Order of the Trapezoid's heritage slithers its way out of the German Expressionist cinema and the genre of the *Schauerfilme* ("horror films") produced especially between 1919 (the date of *The Cabinet of Dr. Caligari*) and 1933. This body of work is touted as a significant influence on the past Grand Master Anton Szandor LaVey's vision of the sources and shape of the Order. But the question really is: Was there any actual connection between the German magical scene and the films of the period? Or were these images merely the products of the film makers' imaginations? We are very much used to seeing uninformed mumbo-jumbo on the screen in more current films. Was it all that much different then? There are those notable exceptions to this general state of affairs: *Rosemary's Baby*, *The Devil's Rain*, and even *The Asylum of Satan*. In those cases, the sources are given credit and it is easy to separate the wheat from the chaff.

Was LaVey's understanding of practical Black Magical precepts that he saw in these films another example of his genius seeing things that were perhaps not consciously intended, or intended only in some Lesser Black Magical way? Another example of this process would be his transformation of William Mortensen's "Command to Look" from, what was after all mainly intended as an effective way of composing photographs, into a Greater Black Magical principle. Or were these images the visible reflections of some Black Order of Satanists working in Germany at the time?

The story of LaVey's first exposure to these films which were to shape much of his vision of the Trapezoid is ambiguously recorded in *The Devil's Avenger* (pp. 27-28.):

> During the summer of 1945, one of Tony's [LaVey's] uncles was hired by the Army as a civil engineer to reconstruct air strips in Germany. Since the uncle had just been divorced he had a family visa opening that was to have been filled by his wife. Instead, Tony went with him.
>
> One day at the command post in Berlin where his uncle was stationed, Tony attended the showing of some German films confiscated from the Nazi's motion picture production office. The movies that interested Tony the most were the

Schauerfilme such as *The Testament of Dr. Mabuse*, about a mad hypnotist and depravity in high and low places in pre-Hitler Germany; and *Metropolis*, about a wizard-scientist named Rotwang who confounds a revolt of slave-like workers by sending a humanoid to double for the Joan of Arc-type of woman serving as the workers' leader. One of the *Schauerfilme* told the story of an effete young man, the scion of a multi-millionaire family of munitions-makers, who entertained his friends with Black Masses. The particular Black Mass favored by this wealthy young German made use of a trapezoid suspended from the ceiling, a revolving pentagon or mirrors, creepy electronic organ music, and electric lights buzzing through his black chapel. A German interpreting the films for the viewing Army brass explained that what they were seeing was not merely fiction, but an authentic representation of a ceremony performed by the Black Order, a secret society of Satan-worshippers. Did such people really exist?

Indeed! Did such people really exist? The question is not answered clearly elsewhere. Later in the same text, it is said with regard to LaVey's early assessment of Aleister Crowley: "Crowley, in some parts of his books, seemed to be the nearest living facsimile to the Black Mass celebrants depicted in the German *Schauerfilm* Tony had seen in Berlin" (p. 32.). The tenuous connection between Crowley and these films may prove more meaningful later. One significant problem remains as to the identity of the exact film in which the Trapezoidal Black Mass is supposed to have appeared. [The best research to date indicates that no such film exists, or has actually survived.]. However, it is certain that LaVey made contact with the emerging Trapezoidal magical stream through Expressionistic films— at least by his own account.

The glaring question remains: "Did such people actually exist?" In order to get the answer one would obviously have to have intimate knowledge of the German occult scene during the years in question. This is a difficult task for anyone not associated with it at that time, as the German magical culture has tended to be considerably more secretive than its Anglo-American counterpart. However, any solid connection between the self-consciously magical culture and that of the film industry (especially the creative forces behind the set designs) would be a good start. This beginning has been provided, I believe, in the person of Albin Grau.

Grau, with the magical initiatory name Frater Pacitius, was the "Master of the Chair" and Master of the Orient Berlin of an order calling itself the Pansophical Lodge of the Light-Seeking Brothers, Orient Berlin. This lodge was constituted in 1921. Its Grand Master was Heinrich Tränker (Frater Recnartus), its General Secretary was Gregor A. Gregorius (= Eugen Grosche). In 1925 a sort of "secret conference" was called at Weida in Germany. The purpose of this conference was to decide whether or not to follow the Law of Thelêma proclaimed by Τω Μεγα Θηριον. The Weida-conference was attended by Tränker and his personal secretary Karl Germer, Grau, Gregorius, Crowley, Lea Hirsig, Martha Küntzel and Norman Mudd. The conference was split and eventually Tränker and Grau (and thus the Pansophical Lodge) decided not to follow the Law of Thelêma. On the other hand, Gregor A. Gregorius accepted the New Æon, and eventually in 1928 founded a Thelemite order known as the *Fraternitas Saturni* ("the Brotherhood of Saturn").[1] The FS was (and is) Thelemite, but was nevertheless independent of Crowley's personal authority. This order has many sinister angles— among them the only references I have seen in older traditional occult literature to Tesla energy and the use of electrical apparatus in magical workings.

So who was this Albin Grau? A review of the credits of major *Schauerfilme* of the period, mostly made at the UFA studios in Berlin, reveal that he was the set designer for such films as *Nosferatu: Eine Synphonie des Grauens* (1921), and *Schatten* (Warning Shadows) (1923). Grau also provided the story line for the latter film which involves a magician who hypnotizes people, and who then "entices their shadows from them causing them to perform the roles inspired by [his] shadow play, acting out their subconscious impulses in a collective dream."[2] Unfortunately, this film survives only in a fragmentary state. But the main point, from our perspective, is that a positive and definite link is established between the world of the makers of the *Schauerfilme* and the occult elite of Germany of that time. Whether as a glorification or villainization, these portrayals these film makers put on the screen can be trusted to reflect some actual magical practice. Generally these Satanic illustrations are usually meant to condemn the factions being portrayed in that light., However, some of the people working on the films must have known something about the nature of this underground. If LaVey was guessing that occult secrets were displayed on these flickering screens, perhaps it can be said he was correct.

There still needs to be further research into the lives and possible occult backgrounds or connections of other set designers of these films, including the fairly well-known Hans Poelzig (*The Golem*), Hermann Warm (*Caligari*), Robert Dietrich (*Homoculus*), Otto Hunte (*Metropolis* and the Mabuse films).

[2019: The contents of this essay will be greatly expanded in the texts of my *Hidden Dimensions of Gothick Horror* and *Gothick Meditations at Midnight*.]

---

[1] See Stephen E. Flowers *The Fraternitas Saturni* (Rochester: Inner Traditions, 2018, 4th ed.), p. 33.
[2] John D. Barlow *German Expressionist Film* (Boston: Twyane, 1982), p. 95.

AUSTIN OSMAN SPARE
AND THE TRACK OF THE TRAPEZOID
(*Runes* V:2 1987)

Mystery and chaos surround the magic of Austin Osman Spare. Spare (1886-1956) was a contemporary of Aleister Crowley with whom he shared several magical interests. Although Spare was formally involved with Crowley's . For a while (around 1910), the two magicians ultimately went their separate ways. Spare began his career as an artist in a promising enough fashion with several published works and one-man shows. But he abhorred established society and spent most of his life (ca. 1930-1956) in a reclusive existence eking out a living selling his drawings in the slums of South London. Toward the end of his life he became involved with Kenneth Grant whom Spare made the executor of his estate. AOS is the subject of one of Grant's more lucid texts: *The Images and Oracles of Austin Osman Spare* (London: Muller, 1975).

Spare worked a peculiar kind of highly personalized magic. One of the main features of his technique was "sigilization." This topic has been most exhaustively and practically treated by Frater U.·.D.·. in *Practical Sigil Magic* (St. Paul: Llewellyn, 1990). Spare used his images as storehouses for his will and as gateways to other dimensions and realities. Spare himself seemed only vaguely aware of the geometrical principles behind much of his work, and his executor and chief interpreter, Kenneth Grant, seems totally unaware of the Trapezoidal implications of Spare's contribution.

The methods Spare used to work with these sigils was largely auto-erotic (cf. VIII° O.T.O.). Spare's utilization of this technique of turning this "Love under Will" upon the Self as its object caused Crowley to assess Spare as a Black Brother— or a "Brother of the Left-Hand Path."

A reading of *The Images and Oracles of Austin Osman Spare* reveals some astounding evidence for the emergence of the Trapezoid in Spare's magical work. At one point toward the end of his life, Spare is said "to have discovered a mathematical formula to express the ultimate development of the Neither-Neither theory..." (Neither-Neither theory is an expression of magical "inbetweenness"— a state between all polarities.) Apparently AOS was very interested in the explorations of other dimensions.

Although he was probably quite capable of fairly sophisticated mathematical theorizing (Grant reports that Spare won the national Gold Medal for Mathematics with a treatise on solid geometry when he was fifteen), his work with extra-dimensional reality seems to have survived mainly in his graphic representations. He committed little to nothing of this kind of theory to paper. Grant does indicate, with little understanding, that Spare spoke of visions and dreams "of extraordinary perspectives which he found himself unable to draw."

Concerning Spare's magical artistic technique, one paragraph in Grant's book is worth quoting in its entirety:

> The unusual perspectives characteristic of some of Spare's work is due to a coordination of time and space. "The only way I can do this [i.e. coordinate time and space] is by a reorientation and the use of two perspectives simultaneously. It is like looking at a person from two different places at the same time." One of Spare's aesthetic theories is that "through attenuation, either horizontal, perpendicular or oblique, there occurs a natural emphasis of the rhythm of aesthetic values inherent in form but usually obscured." By combining two or more perspectives in one object he hoped to reveal its hidden meaning and to evoke its latent power. (p. 13.)

Many of Spare's magical drawings reveal his use of n-dimensional or non-Euclidean geometries for operative purposes. One of the more interesting is reproduced in the work entitled "Aerial Vampire." In this piece we see Spare's use of sigilization coupled with pictographic representations in a matrix of weird geometry. Note also the use of sigils that appear to represent Klein bottle-like shapes.) Spare was certainly one of the first to take mystical approaches to extra- or ultra-dimensional reality into the realm of operative magic.

One of the most curious aspects of Spare's apparent intuiting of the emerging Trapezoidal current is also reported by Grant:

> Towards the end of his life Spare painted witches and ghouls on radio baffle-boards that clients had left with him for this purpose. Some of these in an unfinished state, lay about the room. His landlady switched on some of the radios and a thin distorted sound, wheezing and grating as if forced from the metallic breast of a mechanized ghost, swelled, faded, swelled again, as the volume of the various instruments vacillated in a kind of temperamental storm. (p. 35.)

It seems highly likely to me that these were magical experiments in the same current as later expressed by Anton LaVey's *Elektrische Vorspiele* and Sir Roger's "Tonal Angularity." Again, Grant seems to be totally oblivious to the probable magical utility of these instruments. The sigilic system created by AOS was particular to his subjective universe, but he was working with principles that form gateways into an "Obscene Angle" of the objective universe. Knights and Dames of the Order of the Trapezoid are urged to experiment with original geometrical sigils as gateways to magical spheres in the subjective and/or objective universes— and even into the omnijective vortex between the two. It has long seemed reasonable and practical to me that the daimonic sigils used in goetic magic or the *galdrastafir* used in Runecraft are actually such ultradimensional "keys" to unlock the gates to other realms of reality and causality. I might also suggest that the Trapezoidal magician could use computer graphics or three-dimensional models of ultradimensional space for the same ends to which two-dimensional models (i.e. sigils) were utilized in the past.

MAGIE UND MANIPULATION
(*Runes* V:3 1987)

I

Introduction

In Anton Szandor LaVey's introduction to the ritual he called *Die elektrischen Vorspiele* ("the Electrical Preludes") in *The Satanic Rituals*, he said "The rite, as presented here, was intended to alter an existing social climate and establish far-reaching change." (p. 108) It has long been thought that what the National Socialists were able to accomplish in the field of the politics of power was somehow aided by magical means. The image of cells of the "Black Order" performing versions of this Greater Black Magical *DeV* Working to influence the German body politic is an intriguing one. The reality of this image, in all its technical details, remains one of the chief concerns of the Order of the Trapezoid. This image is also echoed in LaVey's discussion of the Yezidis' Seven Towers of Satan — six of them trapezoidal in form — "intended to serve as a 'power house' from whence a Satanic magician could beam his will to the 'descendants of Adam,' and influence human events in the outside world." (p. 151) Both of these feature the idea of influencing the general social/human environment by means of Greater Black Magic.

As far as National Socialist use of magic is concerned, much of the private work undertaken in the *Ordensburgen* was kept totally secret and any and all documents relating to it were destroyed before the end of the war. Subjective evidence also would indicate that those individuals with intimate knowledge of this work did not survive the war. However, as any effective magician knows, Greater Black Magic aimed at causing effects in the objective universe must, in order to be most reliable, be supplemented with Lesser Black Magical techniques. Of this Lesser Black Magic used by the Nazis we have ample evidence. The subject of this study is the LBM practices of the NSDAP (National-Socialist German Workers' Party) which took the shape of cultic rites. These were used to forge the nation together and to shape and direct the "general Will" of the *Volk*. These cultic rites took many forms, e.g. party rallies, national celebrations, as well as more openly cultic celebrations. The Nazis, for example, instituted a "Morning Celebration" obviously meant to replace church services.

So much mumbo-jumbo has been written about "occult Nazism," I can hear cautious readers now beginning to protest. Happily, with this branch of the study we have several good, reliable sources. The principal two I have used here are George L. Mosse *The Nationalization of the Masses* (New York: New American Library, 1975), and Klaus Vondung *Magie und Manipulation: Ideologischer Kult und politische Religion des Nationalsozialismus* (Göttingen: Vandenhoeck und Ruprecht, 1971).

By the way, Mosse is probably the premier scholar of "Nazi culture," with other books entitled *The Crisis of German Ideology: Intellectual Origins of the Third Reich* (New York: Grosset and Dunlap, 1964) and *Nazi Culture* (New York: Grosset and Dunlap, 1966).

One needs only to see Leni Riefenstahl's *Triumph des Willens* ("Triumph of the Will") to be convinced of the cultic aspects of National Socialist (NS) political rallies. But this aspect was not one that was unconscious or haphazard. The National Socialists willfully set out to establish a national cult which was intended in part to replace Christianity. All the sources on this phenomenon make this quite clear. What is more, each emphasizes at one point or another the magical aspect of these rites, i.e. that they were intended to mold the masses into an instrument of the will of the leader(s). This will is usually seen as an expression of the "general will" of the *Volk*— an appreciation which is perhaps fundamental to any deep understanding of the "Nazi mythos." Mosse writes:

> The pragmatism of daily politics lay within this cultic framework and for most people was disguised by it. But "disguise" is perhaps the wrong term in this context, for any disguise which utilizes regular liturgical and cultic forms becomes a "magic" believed by both leaders and the people, and it is the reality of this magic with which we are concerned. (1975, p. 15)

From a Black Magical perspective, these workings could be seen as efforts to manipulate the masses to do the will of a Black Magical oligarchy. It is interesting to note that the theme of a mindless mass, or automaton (organic or inorganic), which does the will of its master is one that fascinated the German magical mind of the early part of this century. Think of the famous films of the period with the *golem* of Rabbi Loew, Dr. Caligari's Cesare, and Rotwang's robotrix Ultima Futura. Another theme was, however, the specter of a shadow-self or *Doppelgänger*— this complicates the issue magically by posing the question of the ultimate character of the Self.

But to return to the task at hand, what practical magical purpose does it serve to study these rites of "mass manipulation"? First, it provides a historical understanding of how such a magical operation might be mounted. Perhaps never before or since were magical techniques so widely used to wield as much broad objective power as in Germany-Austria between about 1900 and 1945. Second, beyond this historical-exemplary reason, the study can demonstrate practical aspects of the structuring of group Workings and the organization of Order tradition based on previously functioning models. (Again, these may be the most solid ritual remnants of the National Socialist liturgy.) In addition to these, NS liturgy provides a tremendous study in the ritual use of space (proximic magic), and the melding of traditions of the past with those of the future in a maximally effective and pragmatic way.

Only a brief, but I hope insightful and useful, introduction to these matters can be given here. First, we shall look at a group of ceremonies which represent the Nazi effort to create a new national religion. Then we will examine the general structural features of NS liturgy used for almost every purpose.

II
Rites of the NSDAP

Although the NSDAP and all its various groupings, e.g. the SS and the Hitler-Youth, had many kinds of rituals and festivals, we will concentrate here on the more public ones. Of these, there is some public record which can be observed and used by those of us who study these liturgical forms for what we can usefully recover from them. As for the other, more private, or secret, rituals— we are dependent on written records or in most cases the record has been totally lost. By the way, the official Nazi organ for the publication of its new religion was called the *Neue Gemeinschaft* ("New Community").

In the discussions of the various calendrical rites we get a well-rounded picture of the kind of rituals the Nazis were developing. Besides the "Ceremonies of the Reich and the Course of the Year," other liturgical formats used by the NSDAP were: "Morning Ceremonies" ("*Morgenfeiern*") also called "philosophical hours of celebration," or "Ceremonies of Life" (rites of passage), and the dramatic celebratory plays and so-called *Thing*-plays. This latter type of ritual was an effort to create a mass drama in which the audience, or congregation, participated in poetic chants with actors or choral groups. Special open-air theaters, called *Thingstätten* ("Thing-steads") were built for this purpose in the early years of the Reich. These might even be seen as a more "protestant" style liturgy answering to the more "catholic" style practiced at Bayreuth [in the Wagnerian *Gesamtkunstwerke*] where the sacred action takes place in a transcendent space— with only spiritual participation by the audience (congregation).

Right from the beginning we want to avoid the mistake of assuming this liturgy was a completely standardized one, or that it was ever fully developed during the short history of Nazism. Some features were developed only late (after the war had begun) and others fell away in the early years. Some ceremonial forms were practiced only in one or another segment of the Party— which despite the overwhelming *Führerprinzip* was far from a monolithic entity. There was, in fact, a deep æsthetic-ceremonial rift between proponents of a Romantic-Germanic style (favored by *Reichsführer* ᛋᛋ Heinrich Himmler and philosophically by chief National Socialist ideologue Alfred Rosenberg) within the SS and especially within the Hitler-Youth, and a Neo-Classical style favored by Hitler himself (and hence the "mainstream" of the NSDAP).

Ceremonies of the Reich and Course of the Year

It was clear from the beginning of the Third Reich that the Party was actively trying to displace Christianity. One of the most significant ways it set about doing this was through the institution of its own "sacred calendar." The main days celebrated were:

1) January 30: Day of Coming to Power
The principal liturgical act was the night-time torchlight parade as a re-enactment of the one that night in 1933. Its significance was the final victory of the Party.

2) February 24: Proclamation of the Party Program
This was, in the early years, principally celebrated by Hitler and the "Old Guard" in the Hofbräuhaus in Munich in private ceremonies (in which they wore "historical" clothing). It was in the main hall of the Hofbräuhaus that Hitler had first proclaimed the program of the Party on this date in 1920. This was only briefly a special day of public celebration (1934-1935). Its significance was the mythic foundations of victory— which would come to its fruition on the [following] January 30.

3) March 16: Heroes' Memorial Day
This holiday was taken from the Weimar Republic and was originally called "Day of Popular Mourning" (*Volkstrauertag*)— and was a day for mourning the dead of the (First) World War. But it was Nazified into a day of heroic celebration of those who have fallen in battle. The function of this day was national consolation "for those who have not died in vain" much as in the American Memorial Day.

4) Last Sunday in March: Pledging of the Youth
This was analogous to confirmation in the Christian churches. It was the day on which the fourteen year-old boys and ten year-old girls could transfer to the Hitler-Youth (*Hitler-Jugend*) or to the League of German Girls (*Bund Deutscher Mädel*) from the corresponding "junior leagues" of these organizations. Even though this was obviously an individual rite of passage, it nevertheless had national significance as a time of celebrating the commitment of youth to the movement. Liturgically this was principally a private affair handled on a local basis.

5) April 20: Hitler's Birthday
This was never (or only once) a legal holiday, but three important liturgical events took place on this day: 1) The acceptance of ten year-olds in the German Youth-Folk (for boys) and in the League of Young Girls (for girls), 2) The swearing in of Political Leaders of the Party (this took place in full liturgical splendor at night in the Königsplatz in Munich illuminated by torches and vessels of fire) and 3) Military parades.

6) May 1: National Day of Celebration of the German People
Here is an example of a clear usurpation of the Internationalist-Marxist "workers' day" celebration. Although the name of the holiday was changed, the emphasis remained on work and the worker. This was declared the highest holiday of the German people by Goebbels. The German Workers Front liked to fill out the celebration with old Germanic folk customs and celebrated it as the "day of joy over the victory of eternally new life." The day was celebrated widely and officially in Berlin.

7) German Easter and High May
Two days that had taken on Christian importance, Easter, and Pentecost (fifty days after Easter) called "High May" in the folk tradition — were re-paganized by the Nazis. These were celebrated with neo-Germanic festivities and had the function of focusing the attention of the folk on their national heritage as distinct from the internationalist Christianity.

8) Second Sunday in May: Mothers' Day
The ceremonial features of this day were that, after the war had begun in 1939, mothers who had borne a certain number of children were invested with a cross of honor and that those mothers who had lost children in the fighting were taken by flower-bearing Hitler-Youth to the ceremonies where they received places of honor. The apparent function of this day soon became the psychological bolstering of the domestic home-front.

9) June 21: Summer Solstice
This was especially celebrated by the Hitler-Youth and the SS, who seem to have been the two groups in the party most interested in Germanic traditions. In the SS this was the time when good Aryan marriages were made, and various other neo-Germanic festivals were held in several groups. Even Goebbels got in on the act—but without the neo-Germanic trappings. (Neo-Germanicism was more the taste of

Rosenberg and Himmler.) Central to the liturgy of the Summer Solstice was the lighting of the solstice fire. The Olympia Stadium was the central location of this rite after 1937. Its function was again a *völkisch* one— with an emphasis on racial victory. This was a fire ceremony carried out — as usual — at night.

10) First Half of September: Party Day of the Reich
This was the most important celebration of the full power of the Party— the triumph of its will, as it were. Actually, this consisted of an entire week of ritual events. These are the rites that Leni Riefenstahl recorded in her famous documentary film in 1934. These were truly the "high unholy nights" of the National Socialist Party in which every branch and root of its structure took part. Later in this article I will go into some detail on the structure of the rites performed during these days.

11) Beginning of October: Harvest Thanksgiving Day
As May 1 was the workers' day, this was the day to honor the farmer, who held a high position in the Nazi *Blut und Boden* ("blood and soil") ideology. The Harvest Festival Rally was held in the 1930s in the town of Bückeberg near Hameln. Hundreds of thousands of German farmers were brought to this festival which also had a set liturgy, the high-point of which was the presentation of the harvest crown to the *Führer*. This constituted a symbolic presentation of the harvest to the entire community of the *Volk*. In local festivals a similar ritual was carried out in which a high Party official was presented with the symbol of the harvest.

12) November 9: Memorial Day for the Fallen of the Movement.
This is the anniversary of the failed *putsch* of 1923. By all accounts this was the most religiously loaded cultic affair of the Party. The ritual went like this: The "Old Guard," i.e. those who had been there on that day in 1923, and who had been invested with a special medal — the *Blutorden* — by Hitler, gathered with the *Führer* before the *Bürgerbräukeller* beer-hall and marched toward the *Feldherrnhalle*, where sixteen of their number were felled by gunshot. This march was led by those Old Fighters of the *Blutorden* bearing before them the famed "Blood-Flag" (one carried on that day and stained with the blood of the slain). As they marched they passed the pylons upon which were written the names of 240 "fallen of the movement." As the front of the march passed these pylons the names of the martyrs were called out. Throughout this procession, the *Horst-Wessel-Lied* blared through loudspeakers. When they reached the *Feldherrnhalle* sixteen canon shots rang out to commemorate the sixteen deadly shots of 1923. Hitler laid a wreath on the memorial stone of the martyrs, as the *Lied vom guten Kameraden* followed by the *Deutschlandlied* ("Deutschland, Deutschland, über alles...")

which swelled in intensity as the marchers continued their way to the Königsplatz— where the sixteen martyrs had been entombed in the "Temple of Honor." Here a speech — usually by Propaganda Minister Joseph Goebbels — was made. The names of the martyrs were read out as the gathered Hitler-Youth answered chorally— "Here!" After every name there were three-gun salutes. The *Horst-Wessel-Lied* was again played, followed by the *Badenweiler* March and the *Deutschlandlied*.

During the war, this holiday became more of a general day of remembrance for all the dead ancestors as the Nazis tried to displace Christian memorial days that fell in the same season.

13) December 21 and the "Holy Nights"— Winter Solstice

Although already largely pagan in form, the German Christmas festivities became the targets of Nazi liturgical re-interpretation. Himmler was especially interested in re-Germanicizing the festival as the Yule-Fest. Goebbels and Rosenberg both used subtler means. In all cases, however, since this festival had always (even in pagan times) been a private family or clanic and not a public affair, it did not become a candidate for massive Nazi liturgy. It posed a new problem: How to develop National Socialist traditions in private homes. It was 1942 before this began to take on set forms (outside the SS where Himmler's version of the Yule-Fest had long been practiced). The festival was to consist of three major celebrations: 1) of the "troop" (i.e. within NS organizations, military groups, etc.), 2) of the community, and 3) of the family. During the Christmas seasons of 1943 and 1944, the Ministry of Propaganda issued a book called *A German War-Christmas* (*Deutsche Kriegsweihnachten*) which gave a full private liturgy with songs, poems, customs, and legends. This went so far as to present the legend of the dead soldier who returned for the "holy nights" to participate invisibly in the celebrations of the family. (Here again is a purely ancient Germanic belief being revised and revived.)

III
Ritual Formulas

The national Socialist sacred calendar was by no means fully developed— with the outbreak of the war most of the celebrations mentioned above were eventually curtailed quite severely. Some lost their public performance altogether and were reorganized in party cells or in the regular Morning Celebrations (*Morgenfeiern*).

There were many kinds of ritual used by the Nazis, but a common formula underlying at least a portion of most of them, and clearly defining many of them, was a sixteen-point working outline divided into three parts:

Part I:
Fanfares
1. Marching in the Banners and Flags
2. Common Song
3. Poetic Invocation
4. Choral of the Troops (ritualized chants)

Part II:
5. The Eternal Watch (Word of the *Führer*)
6. Choral of the Troops
7. Address of the Highest Ranking Official (*Hoheitsträger*)
8. Honoring of the Fallen
9. Oath of Obligation (to dead, to *Volk*, etc.)
10. Honoring of the Dead (ancestors, heroes, etc.)
11. Choral of the Troops

Part III:
12. Solemn Vows
13. Common Song
14. Honoring of the *Führer* (three-fold *Sieg Heil!*)
15. National Hymns, i.e. the *Horst-Wessel-Lied* and the *Deutschlandlied*

Fanfares
16. Marching Out of the Banners and Flags

Again the question arises— why are we in the Order of the Trapezoid interested in these particular formulas? First, of course, it is part of our mandates, both of the Æon and from Walhalla, to investigate these particular formulas. But from a more widely based magical perspective these rites are useful and practical studies in both Lesser and Greater Black Magic. Like so much else about the "weirder" aspects of National Socialism, these are doubly interesting because they do not constitute some airy fairy, imaginary, or hypothetical "what-if" school of magical thinking, but represent a *Realmagie*. (= *Magia Realia*)

As a form of Lesser Black Magic, these rituals had many functions. Among them were the forging of a focused "general will" of the *Volk*, the creation of a deep sense of self-consciousness as an organic group, the bonding of that group to a set of symbols, the projection of the group through those symbols back in time to the ancestors and forward in time to the descendants— and to ultimate victory. In these mass liturgies the German people were given a direct physical manifestation of the essence of their Walhalla— its spaces, its sounds, its emotions, its powers.

The ritual devices were often complex and manifold, but they generally consisted of these elements: ritually shaped space, motion within that space, color, sound (music) and the spoken word. All this was played out in a pattern of dynamic tension between the individual and the gathered mass— nowhere is this more symbolically clear than the sight of the *Führer* addressing the faithful at Nuremberg.

Every time an individual participates in one of these workings, that person will go forth and act on the emotions evoked during the ritual. In this way each "dynamized" participant goes out and actually re-shapes the world in accordance with the will of the leadership. Shades of Caligari, Rotwang, Mabuse and (gasp!) the Rabbi Loew! All this would appear to have much the same ultimate function as the *Elektrische Vorspiele* as outlined by LaVey— but here making use of certain "psychological resonance" in the masses to effect the magical aims of the leaders. This is reflected in our "culture" by the reason rock bands — motivated solely by profit — will go on tour, even though the tours themselves often lose money. Why? Because the little golems will go out after the "rally" and do the will of their "jukebox heroes" (or their producers), i.e. buy records.

Beyond this Greater Black Magical application, it is also possible that attempts were made to direct these collected energies by means other than "psychological resonance," that is, by means of ritual magic or magical will. These are the type of experiments we have good reason to suspect that the Nazis practiced— but for which we have little hard evidence. Again this is probably because the secret files of the SS, for example, were known to have been destroyed. All we have left are traces and hints, and most importantly, the magical gateways they left open in spaces such as the Hall of the Slain.

A ROOT OF THE "OCCULT NAZI MYTHOS":
Review:
The Occult Causes of the Present War
by Lewis Spence
(*Runes* V:3 1987)

In reading many of the books which deal with the idea of "Nazi occultism" one will sometimes find a reference to this book, published in several editions by Rider in London. Since it was written and published during the Second World War it is one of the earliest published sources of this mythos. It must be counted with the works of Rauschning as the foundation of much of the later literature. When I ordered a copy from a rare book dealer (its last printing was in 1944) I had high hopes of uncovering some new information or at least some leads on further sources. I was encouraged in this hope when I learned that Spence had intimate knowledge of the German occult-magical milieu in the early part of the century, and was in fact an initiate of the German Druidic Order (*Druidenorden*). He had also earlier written a book on Germanic mythology.

The chapter titles of the book seem promising and intriguing enough, i.e. I: The Satanic Element in Nazism, II: The Satanic Power, III: The Satanic Power in Old Germany, IV: Witchcraft, Satanism and the *Vehmgerichte*, V: The Satanic Power in Modern Germany, VI: The Nazi Pagan Doctrine, VII: The Nazi Pagan Church, and VIII: Nazism and Satanism. But when one realizes that the entire purpose and function of the 144 pages of this little book was war-time propaganda, one, pure and simple, one quickly realizes that not much real information will be forthcoming. The book is mainly intended as a polemic against everything German or Germanic.

What is interesting, or at least amusing, from the standpoint of the history of ideas, is Spence's use of circular logic, e.g. the fact that so many witches were burned in Germany is proof positive of the Satanic character of the people. (He sees the churchmen as heroes, preserving "law and order" by the way!) Also, the degree to which Spence himself indulges in what the popular-liberal mind of contemporary society would fashionably condemn as "Nazi thinking," e.g. his disbelief that any "white men" could act as savagely as the Germans, or his analysis of Hitler's character from the shape of his head and face— Spence dismisses him as a "low-grade savage."

In reading the book, one realizes that Spence is not so much opposed to the structures of Nazi thinking as he is outraged by the Germans applying it favorably to themselves. The book is full of statements of British ethnic superiority (especially that of the Celtic Scots— Spence's *own* ethnos, of course). One amusing aspect of this is his insistence that the whole continent of Europe is infected with Satanism— it is common knowledge that the British are too decent and fair-minded to harbor such an infamy!

It is easy to see why this book has never been reprinted after the war. Its title suitably relegates it to the curiosity cabinet of history [— and the author's own racially based logic would discredit the book among its intended audience of today.]

[2019: All matters pertaining to the topic of "Nazi Occultism" will be covered in my extensive study entitled *Nazi Occultism*.]

INFERNAL CONTRAPTIONS
(*Runes* V:4 1987)

Some Initiates might look upon the working and Workings of the Order of the Trapezoid as bewildering exercises in Hollywood (or UFA-Berlin)-style electrical pyrotechnics with little to no relationship to the traditional magical technologies of fire, air, earth and water. They are both right and wrong in this assessment. While it is true that the electrical gismos we sometimes employ as tools in our Workings are essentially non-traditional — that is what they are supposed to be. The Order of the Trapezoid seeks to form a Magick of the Future rooted in the eternities beyond space and time. It is also true that there is a strong cinematic connection in this "Mad Lab" [*Magia Technica*] aspect. The article entitled TRAPEZOIDAL CINEMA (*Runes* V:1 1987) makes it clear that the use of electrical and other mechanical apparati for magical purposes was definitely not simply invented by the imagination of GME Anton LaVey.

Any mention of paranormal applications of technology cannot be made without reference to two men who probably would have been uncomfortable with the label "magician." Nikola Tesla invented many devices that are now used experimentally in a magical context. Principal among these is the so-called Tesla Coil — the magical applications of which are just now being unlocked. Wilhelm Reich invented a device called the Orgone Energy Accumulator which is really a cabinet in which the operator sat. By means of layers of various organic and inorganic substances this was supposed to accumulate a sort of quasi-physical vital energy which was then absorbed by the person sitting in the box.

Within the more self-consciously magical traditions there are two mechanical contraptions of some note that I have come across in the past few years of research.

The first of these is the *prognomètre*. This machine was built by the Polish mathematician-philosopher-magician Joseph Maria Hoëne-Wronski. Hoëne-Wronski was the man who initiated Alphonse Constant, better known as Éliphas Lévi, into the world of magic. Hoëne-Wronski believed that this contraption could "determine the equations of all past, present, and future events, such that it would determine that value of every unknown" according to exact mathematical formulæ based on his theory of the Absolute. A description of this machine is found in *Eliphas Levi: Master of Occultism* by Thomas A. Williams.[‡]

> The divining machine was built at great expense. It consists of two metal globes, one inside the other; turning on a cruciform axis within a large motionless circle, the globes are full of little compartments which open and close, and which contain the principles of all sciences.
> The synthesis of these sciences, classed according to their analogies, is engraved in the double globe which gravitates around two axes . . . On the inner globe which is half light and half dark, one sees written in Wronski's own hand equations for the comparative sciences, and on the large motionless circle the fundamental principles of these sciences are written in the same hand. . .

After Hoëne-Wronski's death, Levi found the *prognomètre* in a junk shop and bought it— although he had no idea of how it was supposed to work. Its present whereabouts are unknown to me.

The second infernal contraption — and one that perhaps deserves the title more than the *prognomètre* — is the dreaded "*Tepaphon*" supposedly first used by the Freemasonic Order of the Golden Centurium (FOGC). The FOGC was founded about 1840, and is supposed to have lasted at least until the 1930s. This is — or was — a Black Magical Lodge of legendary proportions in the annals of German occultism, which was limited to 99 initiates. Membership in the FOGC was in high demand, since it held out the promise of unlimited personal power and wealth to those who would dare to join. Each year they admitted one new member. If none of the 99 had died during the course of that year, the hundredth initiate was sacrificed— quite humanely with poison draught, you understand. But if the chosen sacrifice refused and tried to escape— it did him no good. He could always be killed at a distance by means of the *Tepaphon*. Now you can see why it took guts to join. This machine was used to kill any enemy of the lodge, not just those who refused to "go quietly." The magical autobiography of Franz Bardon, *Frabato*, contains several dramatic depictions of the use of the *Tepaphon*. The machine is also known to initiates of the twentieth century order, Fraternitas Saturni (FS). From descriptions found in FS literature and elsewhere, it can be seen that the *Tepaphon* is an electrical apparatus that projects an arc of electricity into a representative of the victim. It also has moving spiraling attachments which concentrates the will of the magician(s) operating the machine. This acts as a mode of traversing the dimensions of time and space in order that the work be done. It is also worth pointing out that the *Tepaphon* can be used to heal as well as to harm— it is just that destruction rituals make for better stories.

Both the *prognomètre* and the *Tepaphon* can be seen as precursors and fellow travelers when it comes to the equipment used by the Order of the Trapezoid "elektrikal" rites. While the *prognomètre* seems to have been the unique invention of an eccentric magician, the *Tepaphon* is more an example of a magical working tool employed in at least two orders. From all indications it, and machines like it, were the original and informed magical inspiration for the "Mad Lab" scenes found in Expressionistic German films.

‡ (University, AL: University of Alabama Press, 1975), p. 69.

GALDR OK SEIÐR
(*Runes* VI:6 1988)

This article is substantially revised from one I wrote to be included in *The Encyclopedia of the Scandinavian Middle Ages* which will be published by the Garland Press. Here, I will focus more narrowly on the distinction between the kind of magic called *galdr* and that called *seidhr* in Old Norse from a Black Magical perspective. The encyclopedic document of the O∴T∴ is to be called *SEIDHR* after one of these kinds of magic. A true understanding of what is meant by these terms could provide significant insight into the various kinds of magic, and thus lead to a more refined practice of them by the Black Magician Working in any idiom.

The scientific definition of magic is a difficult subject, and one that has been debated for decades. The topic is thoroughly reviewed in the Germanic-Scandinavian context by me in *Runes and Magic*. Magic seems to be volitive symbolic behavior to effect or to prevent changes in the environment by means of extraordinary communicative acts with paranormal factors. Magic is a way for certain human beings to make things happen that ordinarily could not be made to happen. It is generally to be distinguished from religion by the fact that the will of the magician is paramount. The magician makes the environment do his bidding, whereas in religion the human community generally attempts to harmonize its behavior with a universal paradigm.

In accounts of Viking Age (ca. 800-1100 CE) magic, there is a self-conscious division between two types of magic: ON *galdr* and ON *seið(r)*. Galdr is derived from the ON verb *gala*: 'to make the sound of a crow or raven,' while the etymology of *seið*(remains somewhat obscure. It too may have something to do with vocal performance, such as singing or chanting. By the Viking Age, however, *seið*(had developed a reputation for being somehow "shameful." In the *Ynglinga saga* (ch. 7) it is related how the Vanic goddess Freyja taught the god Óðinn the art of *seið*(. It may be that *seið*(was thought to be "shameful" or unmanly because it sometimes involved sexual activity, or perhaps more plausibly because it involved the loss of conscious control and induction of trance states. *Galdr* on the other hand appears to be a more straightforward use of symbolic vocal utterances, often accompanied by visible signs, to impress the will of the magician directly onto the environment. The saga literature is rich with accounts of magic of all kinds.

The most discussed aspect of Scandinavian magic in the Middle Ages (ca. 1100-1550) is that of "rune-magic," i.e. the idea that the runes (the graphemes of the early Germanic writing system) were essentially magico-religious tools. Early scholarly literature on this subject suffered from having a theoretically imprecise basis, which, I hope, has been corrected by the publication of *Runes and Magic*. Whether or not runes are in and of themselves magical, they were used almost exclusively for magical ends in the older runic period (from the first to eighth century CE). A review of the inscriptions of this period shows that not a single one of them must be interpreted in a purely secular, non-magical sense. In the younger period (ninth to twelfth century, CE) such profane communications become more common, and in the following medieval period they become more common still.

As far as the theory and practice of magic with runes is concerned, it is clear that this writing system was used as an aid in objectifying the will of the magician in graphic form. Formulas which until the introduction of the runes were perhaps only performed were now vocally made symbolically more objective, and hence more magically effective, by means of writing. The fact that the word used to class these signs, Proto-Germanic *runô*, ON *rún*, seems to have basically come to mean "a secret" or "a mystery," — "something hidden, arcane, occult" — adds to the credibility of those who see something intrinsically magical in the runes. The ultimate and true meaning of the term is yet to be fully articulated. In the history of magic in Scandinavia there seems to have been no set of symbolic behaviors more important than that of vocal performance followed by an execution of a graphic sign or set of signs to reinforce and confirm the will of the magician. In this process the runes became a primary tool of the magician in pre-Christian times.

After the introduction of Christianity into Scandinavia indigenous cultural features, such as the runes, slowly began to erode. In the field of magic there arose a new tradition, inspired by Continental models, of recording magical "recipes" in grimoires, or, as they were commonly called in Icelandic, *galdrabækur* ("books of magic"). The kind of magic practiced from these books is recorded in two significant ways. First, there is the tradition of the Icelandic folk tales having their origins in this period (12th to 17th centuries) in which the exploits of famous magicians who are said to have used such manuals are recounted. Second, there are the few remains of these books themselves. The most complete of these is the so-called *Galdrabók*. I have put together a complete translation of this manuscript, along with similar sections of old grimoires, published by Samuel Weiser. The theoretical basis for the practice of magic in these sources is essentially unchanged from the heathen period. The magician is usually supposed to speak a vocal formula and then draw or carves a special abstract sign called *galdrastafir*, or *galdramyndir* in Old Icelandic. This varies greatly from the standard forms of magic commonly practiced at the same time on the European Continent. In the latter type of magic, supernatural entities are invoked and somehow coerced into doing the bidding of the magician.

NAZI OCCULTISM REVISITED
(*Runes* VI:6 1988)

Versions of the following two articles were written by me as a partial response to an article which appeared in the Fall 1988 issue of *Gnosis* magazine on the theme of "Northern Mysteries." Although the works were solicited by the editor of *Gnosis*, they were ultimately not included in the issue. I feel that each of these pieces speaks to important topics that are often misunderstood within the body of literature purporting to deal with the phenomena of "Nazi occultism." They have been re-edited for this readership.

The Black Magical Reich

By now it is well known that much of what has been written in such books as Trevor Ravenscroft's *The Spear of Destiny* is a combination of sectarian propaganda and pure fantasy. But the questions remain: How a political and cultural force of the character of National Socialism arise in the midst of a highly educated modern society? What was the nature and history of the groups and individuals involved in this dramatic historical episode? These questions seem to be with us always. Of course, this in itself has little to recommend it, as the human mind, especially one full of vague fears anyway, is quite capable of conjuring all sorts of cosmic evils as the media-driven witch-hunts of the late 1980s showed. "His Satanic Majesty" was already being invoked to explain Nazism during the Second World War itself, as Lewis Spence's book *The Occult Causes of the Present War* (1944) illustrates. But what is the exact nature of this Devil, of this evil, of this Black Magic?

To even attempt to answer these questions with any accuracy, little attention can be paid to the proponents' wilder theories— not at least until we have gotten some reasonable perspective on the whole. Anyone who has seriously read any National Socialist writings or propaganda of any kind will know that no overt appeal to evil or "black magical" powers was ever made. On the contrary, their enemies were usually charged with such epithets. Most sensationalistic writers are unable or unwilling to define exactly what "good" and "evil" is in their tales. They simply assume who the bad guys are, and assume that we will go right along with their somnambulistic game.

If the degree of Nazi evil is to be measured by its level of cruelty, then certainly it can be adjudged no more evil than dozens of other political and religious systems in this century alone. Although in our quantified society we may be impressed by the magnitude of numbers, on a moral basis it really matters little whether one million, six million, or ten million innocents were put to death. Why, then, do the

Nazis make such damn good villains? There is actually a score of reasons why this is so, not the least of which is their own sense of "style." The most "diabolical" of them were even fashion-conscious enough to wear black uniforms, with silver skulls and cross-bones, and sinister-looking Runes. But their level of "evil" seems to go beyond all this. It goes to a level to which most critics dare not penetrate— a level beyond "conventional evil" to a now very dangerous realm of moral or even theological evil. In our present-day world many find this dangerous because confrontation with it is fraught with the possibility that, like Luke Skywalker, they may find some essential aspect of themselves lurking deep within it.

Psychologically, it is not uncommon for modern audiences to identify, consciously or unconsciously (and almost always æsthetically) with the black-clad, ruthless, empire-building villain. This ranges from Captain Nemo, to the Wicked Witch of the West, to Dracula, to Maleficent, to Luke's father, Lord Vader. The underlying reason for this is that we sympathize — even though some may feel that they "shouldn't"— with the Faustian Seeker of Knowledge and Power. This Seeker is someone with a sense of a unique and individual grand purpose and meaning in life, and who possesses the will and ability to carry out these plans. The "good guy" is usually boring, because he just wants to maintain the status quo, serve the king, be a "team player," and perhaps restore order where it has been disturbed by the evil machinations of the villain.

True, these examples are all drawn from fiction, but history is also a kind of rational fiction, subjectively reconstructed by historians from the meager "facts" at their disposal. Sometimes this process can even become quite *ir*rational, as we all know. In any event, we have the tendency to understand history and even contemporary events in terms of archetypal paradigms, or myths, shared with the literary world.

True Black Magic sets out not to do the will of God or of Nature (usually one in the same) but to do its own will— a will forged independent of God's laws or against the grain of nature. In this Black Magicians seek to set themselves apart from Nature, apart from the conventional notions of God: to set themselves up as self-directed, independent deities— or at least to evolve in that direction. The quest and practice of this path is the only viable definition of Black Magic in a philosophical or theological sense in either historical or contemporary perspective.

What is perhaps most frightening for many persons contemplating this is the degree to which modern (or post-modern) humanity derives its motivations and values from the Faustian Black Magical model. The White Magician seeks only to do the "will" of some universal (international), transpersonal deity— to harmonize with it and ultimately to become one with it. The Black Magician rebels against this and seeks only to do his or her own will—a will peculiar to him or her. The structural implications of National Socialism are a curious and powerful mix of these two extremes. Its ability to blend them is based in the principle of elitism. To the Nazi, the concept of "God" is replaced by that of the *Volk* ("People" or more pointedly "Race"). The common man was to become one with the will of the *Volk*. The leadership, and most especially the Leader (*Führer*) exercised his personal "will to power" in the extreme. This *Volk*, the collective organic body of the Germanic ethnic stock, aided by its "priests" (the leadership of National Socialism) became the center of the deity— focused as with the individual Black Magician in the individual vehicle. The Nazis were to separate this new "God" from all others, and develop it to a new level of being. If there is a crux to the issue of the nature of "evil" with regard to the Nazis, or to the question of whether they practiced any sort of "black magic," surely this is it. The Nazi represents a race-based nationalistic rebellion against the natural cosmic order (or perhaps "conventional order"), just as the true Black Magician represent that rebellion in the individual ego.

The individual or collective practice of true Black Magic always seems to focus on the model of an internally directed and willed process leading to higher, more powerful or god-like states of being. In this regard, National Socialism can perhaps be called a form of Black Magic in that it set about — against the grain of Nature — to evolve itself into a higher, more powerful god-like race of supermen based on particular national characteristics. But most critics who throw around such terms as "satanic" or "black magical" do so with little understanding of this and thereby seem to be charging the Nazis with little more than excessive cruelty or with just siding against those whom their psychic script writer has provided with white hats. But with some further understanding, the problem of the relationship of Nazism to our concepts of evil becomes enormously more interesting and far more awesome in its implications for anyone who contemplates it beyond its historical importance.

Occult Roots of the Spear-Mythos

When the intrepid investigator begins a descent into the treacherous subterranean fields of occult connections in the world of political phenomena, matters can quickly become so confused and so obscure that the rational mind is soon pushed over what Colin Wilson aptly calls the "boggle threshold." This usually has as much to do with the way in which phenomena are interpreted as with the character of the events themselves.

One political phenomenon that has received more than its share of occult speculation is Nazi Germany. This ranges from war-time propaganda, such as Lewis Spence's *The Occult Causes of the Present War*, to the free-associating mystifications of *The Morning of the Magicians*, to sectarian viewpoints, such as Trevor Ravenscroft's *The Spear of Destiny*. Other works in this category include Angebert's *The Occult and the Third Reich*, and Suster's *Hitler the Occult*

Messiah. As I cannot hope to analyze this complex body of literature here, much less address the larger issues of occult interpretations of political phenomena. I would like to attempt to clarify one approach in just one of these studies.

Ravenscroft, in his now famous work *The Spear of Destiny*, posited a sectarian and esoteric viewpoint that Adolf Hitler was in fact the reincarnation of a certain evil genius, Landulf II. Landulf II was supposedly used as the model for Clinschor in Wolfram von Eschenbach's thirteenth century epic poem *Parzivâl*, and subsequently for Klingsor in Richard Wagner's *Parsifal*. Landulf reached out over the centuries to exert his evil, "black magic" in the modern world.

It has been convincingly demonstrated that most of the "facts" in Ravenscroft's story are actually fabrications, and that is being charitable. If "true" on any level, Ravenscroft's yarn could only be considered somehow "mystically factual." Nicholas Goodrick-Clarke in his *The Occult Roots of Nazism* devotes a whole section to the basic level of fabrication involved in Ravenscroft's book. In Appendix E Goodrick-Clarke notes that Ravenscroft went so far as to make up names, places, dates, and so forth.

But how did this particular version of the modern mythos of "Nazi occultism" originate? The key may perhaps be found in the person of Ravenscroft's supposed mentor, Walter Johannes Stein. Stein was an Anthroposophist who wrote the book *Weltgeschichte im Lichte des heiligen Gral* (World History in the Light of the Holy Grail) in 1928. In turn, the key to unlock Stein's conceptual world is most logically found in the Anthroposophical doctrines of Dr. Rudolf Steiner (1861-1925).

In Ravenscroft's (or Stein's) historical mythos, a special role of wickedness is reserved for the "infamous" Guido von List (1848-1919). Curiously enough, Stein's mentor and the founder of Anthroposophy, Rudolf Steiner, was certainly a personal acquaintance of List, the Armanist founder of early 20th century Runic occultism. They were both part of the same literary circles in Vienna in the late 1880s and early 1890s. My study of Guido von List presented in *The Secret of the Runes* outlines this and other phases of List's career. However, despite the fact that both List and Steiner were open to many of the same influences, e.g. nascent Theosophy, they developed their ideologies in radically different directions.

Guido von List went on to be one of the founding fathers, along with Jörg Lanz von Liebenfels, of a general Pan-Germanic mystical school known collectively as "Ariosophy" (Aryan-Wisdom). Its major tenets are that the root of wisdom and of occult power is housed within the particular racial stock of the "Aryans" (i.e. Indo-European or "Indo-Germanic" peoples) and that the aim of the movement is the evolution (or re-evolution) of the Aryans into a master race of supermen. This school of (originally) occult thought was not represented by any single organization, but was used as a generic term encompassing dozens of groups and orders. Chief among these were the Guido-von-List-Society and the Ordo Novi

Templi headed by Liebenfels. Steiner's development took another direction, but one which explains well why Guido von List and the Ariosophists would become a perfect model of "evil" from the Anthroposophical perspective.

Writing in his study entitled *The Occult Movement in the Nineteenth Century* (pp. 29-30), Steiner says that "right occultism" is that which seeks a spiritual goal for its own sake, identifiable with the universal-human, while "left occultism" is that which seeks "its own special aims." Here Steiner is speaking in terms "right" and "left" more in the sense of the right and left hand paths rather than in political jargon, although this may have had some relevance as well. Steiner, of course, sees himself in the "right," working for the benefit and evolution of the universal-human in Anthroposophy (Human-Wisdom). It is clear that Steiner would have seen heinous "leftward"- leaning tendencies first in Theosophy itself (from which Steiner broke in 1913) and most especially in the widespread and multifaceted "Ariosophical Movement." In the latter, he would have seen to be using occult means to promote the particular interests of a single faction of humanity over all others. This originally occult Ariosophical doctrine was subsequently politicized and made a founding principle of the ideology of National Socialism.

It is fairly obvious that the roots of the sectarian mythology codified in Ravenscroft's book are to be found in the esoteric doctrines of Rudolf Steiner, as interpreted and taught by Walter Johannes Stein to Trevor Ravenscroft. Moreover, it is clear that the notion of the particular form of "Nazi evil" has, for this esoteric school, more to do with the fact that they belong to the spiritual "left"— pursuing their "own particular aims" — rather than to the universal-human "occult right" as envisioned by Steiner. Like certain other occult thinkers of the Right-Hand Path, Steiner made many accurate observations with regard to the character and relative structures of the Right-Hand Path and the Left-Hand Path. However, from the perspective of the Left-Hand Path itself it is obvious which path is the one filled with virtue and power.

[Commentary 1995/XXX]

Subsequent research clearly shows that the esoteric "right" : "left" dichotomy posited by Steiner was carried forth by Walter Johannes Stein in the form of certain universalistic socio-economic theories. Stein esoterically held that the blood of Christ entered the Earth at Golgotha, making the whole Earth the physical *Body of Christ*, and this "esoteric fact" is to be realized through the development of "a world-embracing economy." This economy "directed from a *universal* point of view" is predicated on the dissolution of national frontiers. This world-economy was to be directed by a nebulous body called the "Order of Christ"— presumably a dedicated band of friendly, hard-working government bureaucrats (cf. the IRS, UN, etc.). Stein held that "The creation of a system of World Economy is the real mission of the Anglo-Saxon/Germanic people."[‡] Stein was in fact brought to

England in 1933 by British business magnate Daniel Nicol Dunlap to aid in the operations of the World Power Conference (later known as the World Energy Conference). In England he continued to work— this included acting as an advisor to Winston Churchill (who became a "patient" of Dr. Stein, who was a homeopathic practitioner).

In stark contrast to Stein's universalistic theories of global economy based upon the presence of the transubstantiated blood of Christ in the body of the Earth are the National Socialist economic theories based upon the existence of discreet individual Nations (*Völker*)— who, linked to their own part of the Earth — compete with each other for the world's resources. The NS aim was to establish an economic space (*Lebensraum*) commensurate with their economic power. This economic system would then become fully independent and self-sufficient— remaining apart from the rest of the world economy. The esoteric basis for NS economics is rooted in the idea of Blood and Soil (*Blut und Boden*).

Each of these economic theories talks about Blood and Soil, of course. The esoteric "right" sees a one-world economy with no national borders, the esoteric "left" sees individuated national economies functioning in relative isolation. The "blood" of the "right" is a collective entity — embodied in the notion of a universal Christ and the "soil" is the whole Earth, while the "left" sees the "blood" as a metaphor signifying the Nation (*Volk*) and the "soil" is the physical land or space occupied by that Nation.

These issues — exoteric though their manifestations may appear as they flicker across the television screen on the evening news — are clear and present esoteric realities facing us today.

Again the question is to be posed: Where does the true evil lie?

---

‡ Stein quoted by Charles Lawrie in "'Doctor Stone': Walter Stein and the Holy Grail" (p. 130).

ON THE CHOICE OF A HUMAN SACRIFICE...
(Runes VII:1 1989)

These are the words that begin one of the chapters of *The Satanic Bible* by Anton Szandor LaVey, and they are words which have come back to haunt the Left-Hand Path movement again and again. In writing them, in the context which Dr. LaVey made quite clear, he was and is perfectly justified. However, the recent events in Matamoros coupled with the deep levels of misunderstanding surrounding the whole notion of "sacrifice" and the use to which a Satanist or even neo-pagan might put this magical technique needs some historical and philosophical clarification.

This whole question is the subject of a hidden reality which is the true knowledge of what a sacrifice is and what its uses are. An aspect of this hidden reality involves the fact that what is commonly referred to as "sacrifice" in popular jargon in reality comprises two radically different kinds of acts.

At this time we need to be quite clear about what a sacrifice is and what our relationship to the practice is historically and philosophically. In Setian circles the term "sacrifice" is rarely, if ever, used in any context, as most Setians have evolved beyond the stage where such practices are useful — at least as they are commonly understood. But with the constant references to "Satanic" animal and human sacrifices, I thought it would be useful at this time to contribute a study of the technique.

The Two Approaches to Sacrifice

First we should clarify our terms. The English word "sacrifice" is derived from the Latin *sacra-ficium*, which literally means "something which has been made 'sacred'" or "something which has been separated out from the profane." The Anglo-Saxons had a whole nomenclature for "sacrifice" also, but most all of them would only confirm what seems to have been a common Indo-European attitude toward the practice of sacrifice, i.e. that it was a holy *gift* to a god and that it was *at the same time* a gift in *return* to the populace worshipping (i.e. honoring) that god. Examples will make this concept clear. Radically different from this conception is that held among other peoples, notably the ancient Hebrews and Aztecs (just to name two). For them "sacrifice" was exclusive payment to a god for favors granted or as a mode of expiating sin. This latter concept has come to dominate our thoughts when we think of sacrifice today. We think of nubile virgins being offered up to the Aztec Sun-God, or the Fire-Goddess Pele in Hawaii. To us now that seems a superstitious waste — which is might well be. The point is that in European culture such a concept was unknown until the introduction of Christianity, and with it the Old Testament lore of the ancient Hebrews.

Because the study of sacrifice is an extremely complex one, even within a given culture, I will limit myself to discussions of the two kinds of sacrifice most in question right now— animal and human. I will concentrate on the forms of sacrifice as practiced by the pre-Christian Germanic peoples from the most ancient times to 600-1100 CE, depending on the region in question.

In the old Germanic conceptual universe, a sacrifice, or more simply, a *gift* to the gods came in two main forms. First there were the animal gifts. Certain animals are thought to embody the essences of certain gods and goddesses, e.g. the swine of Freyr and Freyja, the goat of Thorr, the horse of Óðinn. These animals would be slaughtered by priests in a ceremonial setting, and the meat from the animals would then be eaten by the people in a ceremonial meal. In this way the god is able to commune with his folk in an *essential* way, and they with him. This is not only a gift *to* the god's being, but simultaneously *from* that being. It might also be pointed out that the priests also took great care in making the death of the animal as painless as possible. One Old Norse term for sacrifice is *sóa*, which literally means "to cause to go to sleep," the origin of our current euphemism "to put to sleep." This is important because the animal embodies the god, which is loved by the folk, and thus they would not want to cause it pain. The traditional Indo-European animal sacrifice is in reality a sacramental meal in which the gods and humans symbolically commune. It is worth pointing out that certain parts of the animal are given up to the god in a fashion similar to that of the Hebrews— but these should only be the parts of the animal that were more or less useless to humans— the lower legs or heads.

Another form of sacrifice was the giving of a human being. Generally only two gods, Tyr and Óðinn seemed to have been the recipients of human sacrifice— these were the two most sovereign gods. Tyr is the god of law and justice, while Óðinn is the god of magic, death and wisdom. But far from sacrificing the finest the tribes had to offer, the only persons subjected to being victims of sacrifice were criminals and prisoners of war. The Germanic peoples were notorious for taking no prisoners of war. The religious reason for this is that to them all war was considered a sacred ritual in which all those slain on the other side would be dedicated to the gods (Tyr and Óðinn) and declared to be sacrificial victims even before any actual fighting began. So any prisoners captured would simply have to be taken to the groves sacred to the gods and there be more ceremonially dispatched. Criminals were also often made the victims of human sacrifice. The rationale behind this is that the criminal has violated the natural balance of the cosmos by his actions, and as such forfeits his life to rebalance the wrong. Both the military enemy and the criminal are really considered in the same category — as breakers of the peace — who must repay the wronged god or goddess with their lives.

One other kind of human sacrifice, more seldom encountered for obvious reasons, is the sacrifice of the king. If things were to go especially badly for a kingdom, for example the crops failed repeatedly, or the frontiers were continually unsafe from invasion, the semi-divine king, who was known to some of the Germanic as well as other Indo-European groups, would more or less voluntarily offer himself as a victim of sacrifice in order to rebalance the cosmic order in favor of his people.

If we compare the general Indo-European attitudes toward sacrifice with the ideas contained in the "On the Choice of a Human Sacrifice" text by LaVey, I think we can see that they are virtually the same. LaVey essentially says that those who have wrongfully harmed you to an extreme degree are the prime candidates for "human sacrifice"— through magical, not physical means. In this he is right in line, not only with the traditional ancient thoughts on sacrifice, but also with philosophical proponents of the state imposed death penalty. In the matter of the sacrifice of the god-form in animal shape, LaVey shows no evidence of a desire to make use of this. He is righteously indignant over the thought of sacrificing animals or children for any purpose, as he holds animals and children to be the purest expression of the god-head of carnal existence— as he conceives it.

But what about the model of sacrifice as portrayed in the lurid accounts of the supposed activities of "Satanists"? Where could these depictions have come from if the pagans of Europe did not indeed practice anything like it? The answer is rather simple, but it is one that makes the establishment quite uncomfortable.

Any reading of the so-called Old Testament, or the *Torah* of the Jews will show a highly developed cult of not only animal, but also of human sacrifice. The ancient Hebrews did not share in a convivial meal with their god or gods, but rather offered the animal to him completely. Not only is this attested in the Old Testament, but rules and regulations concerning its practice make up whole parts of the books of Leviticus and Numbers. These books are veritable charnel houses with instructions to make burnt offerings of massive numbers of animals of various kinds. Yahweh must have grown very fat from the glut of burnt flesh the temple priests sent his way in those years.

Although the Jews must have given up the regular practice of human sacrifice at some time, their holy books still have some references to it. The most famous case is the little practical joke Yahweh played on Abraham— where he tells Abraham to sacrifice his only son, Isaac, but stops him at the last minute (Genesis 22). Now this is actually a representation of the fairly common Semitic practice of the "sacrifice of the first fruit" which was at one time extended even to human offspring. But not to leave the girls out: There is also the story of Jephthah (Judges 11) who vowed to offer as a burnt offering to god "whatsoever cometh forth of the doors of [his] house to meet [him]," if god would grant him victory in the war against the "sons of Ammon." Well, after his victory, the first thing that came out of his house to meet him was his only daughter "with timbrels and dances." It seems Jephthah was a better general than he was a logician— what did he think would be coming out of his house— a goat? Anyway, Jephthah made good on his vow to sacrifice his only, and still *virgin* daughter.

These references may be thought to be only isolated cases used to spice up the biblical narrative. But such is not the case. It is well-known that all of the Semitic peoples practiced human sacrifice of the first fruit of the womb at one time or another. The Hebrews included. It is still customary to have to "buy back" the first born son from god. This is still done in a ceremony called the *pidyon ha-ben*— "redemption of the first-son." This originally referred to a human sacrifice, but was later changed to dedicating the son to "temple service." Now the kid can be bought back with a few shekels paid to the *kohen*!

It was also an ancient Semitic belief that sin could be atoned for through the shedding of blood. Thus animal sacrifice was used to "purify" one's self of "sin." this is the essential liturgical drama at the root of the myth of Jesus as seen from a Judaic perspective.

When we look back over all this evidence, a high degree of confusion is possible. This confusion comes about simply because the modern "civilized" European might still hold many of his own heathen ancestors' ideas about the appropriateness of "sacrifice," under whatever name. But at the same time this "civilized" man has been taught that which is overtly and historically heathen is to be rejected as somehow an abomination. Add to this quandary the fact that the old Hebrew patterns of sacrifice were often ignorantly projected by Christians onto ancient historical forms of pre-Christian paganism in Europe. The simple-minded Christian just might have thought that all forms of pre-Christian cult must have been just like the pre-Christian Hebrew cult, and thus Old Testament practices were wrongly ascribed to European pagans. We know that this method of Christian historicizing was quite common.

Also quite common was the tendency for Christian writers to take on Roman descriptions of "paradoxical and degraded" cults — as Tacitus described the Jewish cult — by simply copying the texts, now ascribing to pagans, heretics (including Jews), or devil worshippers the practices formerly (and sometimes accurately) attributed to the Jews and/or Christians. In this way stories of heinous forms of sacrifice, as practiced in the Middle East, were first ascribed to medieval heretics, and have eventually found their way into modern descriptions on sensationalistic and propagandistic television programs and tabloids.

The cruel irony in all this is that the ideology "guilty" of all the apparently unacceptable beliefs and practices is never identified or assailed, while the ideology with the balanced and healthy view has become the target of various forms of bigoted attack. It should not be assumed that I am here criticizing the rights of various cults to practice whatever form of sacrifice they wish, or that historical forms of various religions are being vilified wantonly. It is merely a matter of seeking and finding — using rational and historical means of investigation — the sources of the various patterns we encounter and laying the results of our investigations at the proper doorstep.

Addendum 2019
Meditation on the Seal of Rûna

The Seal of Rûna which appears on the cover of this book is a *personal* Fifth Degree Device of the author. When the first edition of the publically available version of this text was put out, the mysteries of this Seal were still secret and held within the teachings of the Order of the Trapezoid. Many of these secrets have been published in a book by the Grand Master of the Order Toby Chappell in his book *Infernal Geometry* (Inner Traditions, 2019. I was happy to see that the GM of the Order felt that it was time to release some of these concepts, and so I will discourse on the Seal further here.

The seal is built up from three geometrical forms: the Pentagram of Set, a Circle or Ring and a Trapezoid. The Seal of the Nine Angles is a combination of the Trapezoid and Pentagram thus:

I noted that if one placed the Ring around the Pentagram in the manner prescribed by Michael Aquino, i.e. in the precise way in which he designed the Pentagram of Set with the points of the Pentagram not touching the Ring or Circle, but held Isolate within the space defined by the Ring, that once the invisible Trapezoid was made manifest in conjunction with the Pentagram that the profound magical meaning of the Trapezoid is revealed as the gateway or link between the

Principle of Isolate Intelligence, as defined by the Pentagram, and the Ring of Nature from which the Principle is usually isolated. The Trapezoid is the link between Intelligence and Nature— the magical gateway. This linkage is reflective of the Romantic mandate of the Order.

This sign is both an illustrative piece of geometrical philosophy — another of the many possibilities of the Enneagram — and an operative tool of magic. *Infernal Geometry* provides what is Necessary. The Seal of Runa can also be used as a powerful meditative instrument. It is an angular *mandala* (Sanskrit: "circle") as a cosmological map and a *yantra* (Sanskrit: "machine, contraption") as an instrument for causing magical effects.

The secret roots of its meaning were first encoded in a series of *mantras* (Sanskrit: "mental instrument") in Michael Aquino's "Ceremony of the Nine Angles" printed in *The Satanic Rituals* (Avon, 1972). The substance of the contents of Chappell's book constitutes the *tantra* (Sanskrit: "secret myth, tradition, teaching") of the symbol. I use Sanskrit terminology here simply because scholars using that language most completely articulated this process as a science.

To begin to meditate with the Seal look at it in a static fashion with whatever you have learned of it reposing in your mind. The next stage brings it into dynamic circulations as you observe the Seal and trace in your mind's eye the lines that make up the Nine Angles, from point to point, as enumerated here.

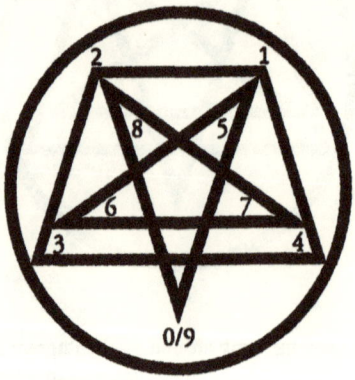

The last phase to be discussed here is to repeat the tracing exercise entirely free of any outward visual stimulation— completely visualized within your mind. See what mysteries will be revealed.

Bibliography

[Bibliographical entries have been brought up to date for this edition. Dates appearing in square brackets indicate the date of the original publication of the first edition of the work in question.]

Angebert, Jean-Michel. *The Occult and the Third Reich*. New York: Macmillan, 1974.

Aquino, Michael. "Evolution of the Order of the Trapezoid Insignia" *Runes* IV:2, pp. 11-16.

———. *Book of Coming Forth by Night: Analysis and Commentary*. San Francisco: Temple of Set, 1985.

———. *The Church of Satan*. San Francisco: Temple of Set, 1989, 2nd ed.

Barlow, John D. *German Expressionist Film*. Boston: Twyane, 1982.

Chappell, Toby. *Infernal Geometry*. Rochester: Inner Traditions, 2019.

Flowers, Stephen E. *Runes and Magic*. Bastrop: Lodestar, 2014, 3rd ed.

———. *The Galdrabók*. Smithville: Rûna-Raven 2005, 2nd ed.

———. *The Fraternitas Saturni*. Rochester: Inner Traditions, 2018, 4th ed.

———. *Lords of the Left-Hand Path: A History of Spiritual Dissent*. [Privately printed MS, 1994.]

———. *Blue Rûna*. Bastrop: Lodestar, 2001.

———. *Lords of the Left-Hand Path*. Rochester: Inner Traditions, 2012.

———. **Wôðanaz: Our Ancestral God of Sovereign Wisdom*. (Rune-Gild/Woodharrow White Paper). Bastrop: Runestar, 2018.

Frater U∴D∴ *Practical Sigil Magic*. St. Paul: Llewellyn, 1990.

Goodrick-Clarke, Nicholas *The Occult Roots of Nazism*. Wellingborough, UK: Aquarian, 1985.

Grant, Kenneth. *The Images and Oracles of Austin Osman Spare*. London: Muller, 1975.

Hall, Edward T. *The Hidden Dimension*. Garden City, NY: Anchor, 1969.

Hollander, Lee M. ed., trans. *Poetic Edda*. Austin: University of Texas Press, 1962.

LaVey, Anton Szandor. *The Satanic Bible*. New York: Avon, 1969.

———. *The Satanic Rituals*. New York: Avon, 1972.

Lawrie, Charles. "'Doctor Stone': Walter Stein and the Holy Grail." In: Matthews, John, ed. *The Household of the Grail*. Wellingborough: Aquarian, 1990, pp. 120-136.
List, Guido von. *The Secret of the Runes*. trans. Stephen E. Flowers. Rochester: Destiny, 1988.
Littleton, C. Scott and Linda A. Malcor. *From Scythia to Camelot*. New York: Garland, 2000.
Mortensen, William. *The Command to Look: A Formula for Picture Success*. San Francisco: Camera Craft Publishing C., 1945. [Originally published 1937.]
──────────. *The Command to Look: A Master Photographer's Method for Controlling the Human Gaze*. Port Townsend: Feral House, 2014.
Mosse, George L. *Nazi Culture*. New York: Grosset and Dunlap, 1966.
Mosse, George L. *The Crisis of German Ideology: Intellectual Origins of the Third Reich*. New York: Grosset and Dunlap, 1964.
Mosse, George L. *The Nationalization of the Masses* (New York: New American Library, 1975.
Ravenscroft, Trevor. *The Spear of Destiny*. New York: G.P. Putnam's Sons, 1973.
Schäfer, H.-W. "Wolfram's *calix lapideus*" *Zeitschrift für deutsche Philologie* 103 [1984], pp. 370-377.
Spanuth, Jürgen. *Atlantis of the North*. New York: Van Norstrand Reinhold, 1979.
Spence, Lewis. *The Occult Causes of the Present War*. London: Rider, 1944.
Stein, Walter Johannes. *Weltgeschichte im Lichte des heiligen Gral*. Stuttgart: Orient-Occident Verlag, 1928
Steiner, Rudolf. *The Occult Movement in the Nineteenth Century* (London: Rudolf Steiner Press, [1973]
Suster, Gerald. *Hitler the Occult Messiah*. New York: St. Martin's Press, 1981.
Thorsson, Edred. *Rune Might*. Rochester: Inner Traditions, 2018.
──────────. *Northern Magic* St. Paul, MN: Llewellyn, 1992.
Vondung, Klaus *Magie und Manipulation: Ideologischer Kult und politische Religion des Nationalsozialismus*. Göttingen: Vandenhoeck und Ruprecht, 1971.
Williams, Thomas A. *Eliphas Levi: Master of Occultism*. University, AL: University of Alabama Press, 1975.
Wolfe, Burton. *The Devil's Avenger*. New York: Pyramid, 1974.
Wolfram von Eschenbach. *Parzival*. trans. H. Mustard and C. Passage. New York: Vintage, 1961.

Notice

Entry into the Order of the Trapezoid is only possible for members of the Temple of Set who have attained the Grade of Adept within the Temple's Initiatory structure. For more information on the Temple of Set, contact may be gained through correspondence with the Executive Director, Post Office Box 470307, San Francisco, California 94147 or contact at the website www.xper.org.

www.ingramcontent.com/pod-product-compliance
Lightning Source LLC
Chambersburg PA
CBHW020213090426
42734CB00008B/1049